Published by One Door Press.

# ONE DOOR PRESS

Image Courtesy: Subbotina

Malene Jorgensen – How to Start a Beauty Blog: Building a Beauty Empire Online

ISBN-Print: 978-1-77181-012-8

ISBN-E-Book: 978-1-77181-013-5

# Disclaimer

Though the author has used her best efforts in preparing this book, she makes no representations or warranties with respect to the accuracy or overall completeness of topics covered in this book, as strategies for web content do change over time.

The advice and strategies contained herein may not be suitable for all business situations, including your own. Consult with a professional before making any changes where appropriate to better your business. This book is meant to be informative and educational at best.

Neither the author nor the publishers shall be held liable for any loss of profit or any commercial damages, including but not limited to special, incidental, consequential or other damages.

# A Note from the Author

My goal with this book is to separate the fashion industry from the beauty industry when it comes to blogging and online content. These two industries are often lumped into one, but you don't have to write about fashion to get the most out of beauty blogging, especially if your interests solely include facial creams and lipstick shades. Let me show you how you can get the most out of beauty blogging.

*This book is dedicated to my family – the ones who let me do the crazy things I do – even when they are indeed crazy.*

# Table of Contents

# Introduction

*"Love of beauty is taste. The creation of beauty is art"* –
*Ralph Waldo Emerson*

The beauty industry is huge, because most of the products and services available are dedicated to improving oneself, whether you are talking about facial creams, wrinkle creams or makeup. And people always want to look and feel their best. And yet, there are not many websites solely dedicated to beauty. In fact, the beauty industry isn't very big online – at least when it comes to blogging, even though it is huge in retail. Beauty is often a small part of a larger website, whether the site aims to target celebrity news or fashion. For example, the PEOPLE magazine website has a section dedicated to celebrity beauty, even though the main purpose is to provide celebrity news. Some fashion blogs will include beauty segments which cover red carpet events, where the stars get ready for a great photo opportunity. And while major websites will contribute a section to beauty, it is rare you will find one website dedicated to just beauty reviews, products and news.

So, why are people not writing about the beauty industry? Well, many people go to the store if they want a product. They can just ask a store clerk for help if they want more information about the product in question before actually buying it. It is essentially a one-stop shop. However, an increasing amount of people are shopping online for products - electronics, clothes and music. It is only a matter of time before people will seek professional advice online about what beauty products to purchase to deal with skin issues, wrinkles or even makeup. Sure, people still search for advice and information online, but many head to the store to actually buy the product. At present time, the beauty industry has over $150 billion in sales per year worldwide. Why wouldn't you want to get involved?

Since beauty products are often incorporated into the fashion industry on major websites, it can be hard for beginners to distinguish what "beauty" entails. Beauty is not the look on a fashion runway. You may think something is beautiful, but that doesn't mean it falls under "beauty." It is not how a person feels carrying the newest handbags. Instead, it is all about the products that make a person feel and look the best in terms of creams, nails, and hair. One way to think of it is imagining a person in the nude. What products can you apply or use on the person that could improve his or her feelings about him or herself that do not include clothes, hats, shoes or underwear? Well, cosmetics, perfume, hair products, skin products and salon treatments, such as manicures and pedicures would fall under this category. Some people would argue that the beauty definition should include workout tips, health clubs and cosmetics surgeries.

Now that you have an idea of what the beauty industry entails, let's talk about how you can make this into a blog. I will introduce you to the technical requirements for creating a website and help you with the design part. But you may already have an idea in mind about what you want the blog to represent for your readers. Websites that are solely dedicated to the beauty industry will have several features; how-to articles, video tutorials and product reviews. Websites that focus on something else will have a section for beauty, such as PEOPLE magazine and US Weekly that focus on celebrity news. These sections will often feature press releases about beauty products or beauty regimes that celebrities use to get ready for big events. It is rare that you will find any product reviews or how-to articles for new products on the market on websites that have other directions than beauty.

Since the beauty industry isn't really too prevalent on the internet at present time, new beauty bloggers have an excellent opportunity to create something big. Many websites will dedicate a small chunk of a larger site for beauty news and content, but there are only a few websites available that only tackle beauty content. So, how can you become a major player in this industry by starting a blog? One of the most important things for beauty blogs is to know your blog brand, identity on the web and goals. Let me introduce you to a few beauty blogs so you can see what I mean.

**The Beauty Department:** This website is one of my favourites when it comes to beauty. It is run by two girls, Amy and Kristin, and they focus mostly on tutorials. They have tons of "how-to" articles and their website is very colourful and modern. Amy is all about the makeup tutorials, while Kristin is all about the hair. These girls are all about how to get the most out of your hair and makeup. And this is how they brand the blog. Once you visit the website, you know what to expect from them.

**Elle.com:** Even though Elle Magazine is classified as a fashion magazine, the website does have a rather large beauty section. The site focuses on beauty from the international runway, new beauty trends and addresses beauty myths. You will also be able to find some how-to articles, if the tutorials cover a new trend or a hairstyle that is street-chic, for example. Elle.com truly defines itself as being at the forefront of the beauty industry.

**Daily Glow:** Daily Glow is a newer website that tries to tackle everything in the beauty industry. The website has several sections, including skin and beauty tips, hair care information, personal care, makeover stories, beauty news from larger companies and celebrities, and product reviews. This website is not as niche as the other ones I mentioned in this introduction, but you can find lots of topics on this website. Daily Grow is driven by contributed content, meaning you are reading articles from many different writers with different experiences and knowledge.

This introduction to these existing beauty websites should make you question where your future website will fit in. Will you solely focus on hair tutorials and products? Or will you cover more than one beauty area but only offer how-to articles? Or will you simply offer product reviews? All of these directions can be profitable, so don't think too much about where the money is coming from. It is important that you pick a topic that you are passionate about and can see yourself sticking with for months to come. You don't want to pick a topic you are lusting for now, but lose interest in after just a few weeks. If you are starting a blog with the hopes of making money from it, you will have to invest time into making it worth visiting. And you should educate yourself to the point where you know everything about your topic. In other words, make sure you know exactly what you want to talk about on your beauty blog. If you want to offer a little bit of everything, like Daily Glow, expect to keep yourself very busy.

As you start pondering about what direction you will take with your beauty blog, let me explain what you will learn in this book. First, I will help you create your blog. Signing up for a free one won't do the trick, as you will be very limited. A free blog doesn't give you the same freedom when it comes to advertising, design and search engine optimization. I will guide you through everything you need to know to get started. I will hold your hand through it all.

I will also take you through the content you can provide. There are benefits and downsides to providing all types of content and you should know them so you can narrow down your approach to your topic. I will also teach you where you can find new information for blog posts, so you can stay active on your blog without too much stress.

And since you may have picked up this book in hopes of starting a full-time blog focused on your favourite beauty topics, I will teach you how you can make the most of your blog in terms of money. Making money online is not easy, but there are certain things you can do to make a little bit of money here and there. The bigger your blog becomes, the bigger the chance that you can make some serious money from it. Don't expect to pull in hundreds of dollars during your first week. But don't give up because you see pennies.

If you want to run a big website that everyone goes to for beauty advice, then you must think big. Blogging is just the beginning. There are many people who can make ends meet with blogging alone, but others strive for more. For example, Elle.com isn't just a beauty blog; the beauty section is a piece of a much larger puzzle. I'm not saying that you should strive to become the next Elle with several international offices, but it doesn't hurt to dream a little big. If you have a hard time seeing where blogging can take you, I'll show you some ideas that you can think about as you grow your blog. Your readers may let you know what they are looking for, which could help you determine what direction you need to go.

In other words, you could use this book as a starting point to build a big online empire. I will introduce you to blogging and give you ideas to grow your website even further. I will even help you monetize your content, so you have a chance of making money from it. However, only you can decide where you want to take your online home. If you feel confident and ready to get started, let me guide you through the necessary steps to create a fully functional website, where you have the freedom to grow your beauty blog to the heights you desire.

# Chapter 1: Building a Website

Every blogger requires a website, so before you can even start blogging about beauty, you will need a publishing platform. If you have no experience when it comes to building a website, the thought of reading this next chapter may terrify you a bit. You may have heard that websites are usually designed using code, such as HTML and CSS for styling. And while those components are necessary to make a great website, it is something that you don't necessarily have to deal with directly. There are many programs online that can help you create a website using HTML and CSS without you ever having to edit or create any code.

Let me explain a little; the following sub-chapters will take you through the necessary steps to make yourself a beautiful, modern and fully functional website for your beauty blog. There are three major components to your website; a hosting and publishing platform, a suitable theme, and the steps of pulling the red thread through it all to make everything work. I will help you through these steps. If you have searched online for website builders before, you may have been presented with free options, such as Weebly, Webs and Blogger. If you are just planning on having a platform where you can share your thoughts, then a free option would be great. However, if you want to have the freedom over the design, the advertisement space, the ability to make money and the ability to build your blog towards a large and powerful brand, then you should get your own hosting account.

You may be wondering why some companies can offer you free websites. A free website isn't necessarily free as such. While you don't pay anything in terms of compensation for the site, you are offering some valuable advertising space – and the company keeps all of the advertising income. These advertisements could be damning to your company or brand. For example, if you are writing a make-up tutorial on creating a smoky eye, the last thing you want on your website is an advertisement for pet sitting services. And if you are trying to create a big beauty brand, you want the advertisements to match the content. That way, people are more inclined to click on the advertisement, which is how you make money. In addition, you are also giving away your freedom when it comes to design. Many of these websites only offer a limited amount of templates, meaning your website could look identical to others on the internet, covering various topics.

In addition, free isn't free when it comes to your domain name. You will have to pay for your own domain name on all free website services. The website you are given will be an extension of the original domain – a sub-domain. And there are many technological issues with having a sub-domain. Let's say the website company you are using the host your website is called www.freewebsites.com (this is just an example). Your domain would then become www.beautyforyou.freewebsites.com. In other words, you have to share your domain with the company you are hosting with. A sub-domain may also come off as less professional as you won't be taken seriously as a company. You don't see Elle.com running on a sub-domain, for example. And since it is so easy to create a website, you may lose trust and readers' interests if you don't make that effort.

Once you start reading through this chapter, you may realize that there is also the issue of search engine optimization, also known as SEO, when it comes to the free websites. SEO is the technique of getting your website optimized for searches, so your website will show up in search results more often than other sites, when people are looking for content related to yours. There are many ways to increase your website's occurrence in relevant searches, but SEO heavily relies on the keywords within the content, your domain name and your meta-descriptions. In other words, if you are not in full control of these key components, your website may disappear in results and get squashed by the larger websites that do have full control over these areas. If you are ready to dive right in, let's start with hosting and Wordpress, one of the most user-friendly publishing platforms.

# 1.1 Hosting and Wordpress

As you are starting out with your website development, there are some terms that you will run into repeatedly. If you already have a blog on a free website service, then considering reading through this chapter to see how you can gain more control of your blog by investing in a new website. The free website won't introduce you to the following terms, because you don't need to know what they are because you are not in control of them. I have taken these definitions straight out of my second book, "How to Become a Fashion Writer: Taking Your Writing to the Runway" as they are just as applicable for beauty blogging.

- **Wordpress**: Wordpress is one of the world's biggest tools for creating your own website. Wordpress actually has two options for you. Wordpress.com is for people that wish to start a free blog (you will be forced to use a sub-domain website if you use the free service unless you invest in a domain name. The freedom to do other things would still be limited) and Wordpress.org is where you need to pay for your website. However, you will be gaining your own domain, which is important for branding and professionalism. If you get your own hosting service first, you may not need to remember the two Wordpress sites, as most hosting services will link you to the .org version of Wordpress

- **Hosting**: The best way to describe hosting for beginners is the place where all of your content is stored. Your content isn't just your pictures, your articles and your design; it is everything including the Wordpress platform and domain. If you imagine a Tupperware bowl as the hosting, the food within it is your content. Together, it creates a presentable and contained website. You can't have one without the other in all cases, but sometimes your partial hosting is part of the free service. One without the other is close to useless if you want to make a career out of blogging. If you are going for the free website, you will be allowed to host your content on the Wordpress servers. However, if you plan on having more websites in your future, I suggest going with a hosting account. I will show you how to set everything up with BlueHost.com in the next chapter

- **Themes**: A theme is the basic layout of your website. Some will call it a template. These themes are rather simple and empty when you first install them, but they do give you the freedom to create a custom blog. There are hundreds of websites online that will provide you with themes or templates for the Wordpress platform, meaning you can get your website to look the way you want. You don't have to settle for the basic theme. Themes are priced from $20 up to $50 depending on how professional they look and how many features they offer. If the developer put much more effort into make it easier for you to navigate, expect to pay on the higher end for themes. You can browse through hundreds of themes before making your final decision

- **Plugins**: Plugins are add-ons you can download for your website. The theme you install may just offer the basic layouts of your home page, a contact page, your portfolio and your blog. You may have the freedom to change colors and layouts in terms of sidebars, but the theme may not offer much more if you are buying on the lower end. However, you can download plugins for free to make your website more professional. For example, plugins allow you to install social media buttons to make it easier for your readers to share the content they are reading, allows you to integrate a Twitter feed for your readers to follow, gives you the freedom to manage spam and advertisements, and allows you to fully customize your e-commerce shop if you wanted to integrate one of your website. So, if you feel that you don't get everything you need in a purchased theme, you may find what you are looking for in the downloadable plugins section. I will show you more about that in the next couple of chapters

You may have to refer back to these terms as you read this book and start designing your website. If all of this is new to you, it may feel a bit overwhelming. But as I take you through the technical requirements of setting up a website, you should be thinking about your direction – your niche. You need to figure out what you want to talk about.

In my first book, "How to Start an Internet Business: 7 Ways to Turn Your Passion into Profit," I dedicated a good chunk of the book on niche blogging. The book was essentially a guide on how to make money online and niche blogging is one of the best ways to combine your passion with online profitability. In that book, I didn't talk about beauty as such. It was a general book where you could apply your own niche, if you had one. But let's take a look at niche in terms of beauty. I have altered the following quote from my first book to suit this purpose.

"The term "niche" means that something is very focused and specific. The term has the same meaning when it comes to blogs. Niche blogs are very focused in content. A niche blog is not a blog discussing beauty and fashion, for example. Instead, it is one that discusses hairstyles and hair treatments, or one that talks about eye makeup tutorials. This is where the importance of what, where, who, why, when and how comes into play."

In my fashion book, I talk about the importance of niche because you may have a hard time encouraging people to click on advertisements that promote weight loss even though you are talking about shoes. These advertisements may show up because you are talking about a wide variety of topics, not something specific. That means you are using various keywords to specify your advertisements, resulting in all types of ads. Because advertisements programs often use the words you use in your content to find the proper ads, you want to use the same focused keywords throughout. For example, if you are writing about skin care, the words "skin care" will be prominent throughout your blog posts. However, if you are tackling more beauty products, you will use the words "skin care," "hair care", "facial cream," "makeup," "personal beauty," "nail polish," "makeup" and "cosmetics," which doesn't really help you find focused ads. In fact, you could get plenty of general advertisements. Plus, when you are trying to sell advertisement spots on your website, you may have more success if your content is targeted. A hair care provider may be sceptical of paying your requested fee for an ad spot if only a small percentage of your content was targeted towards hair care. But you may find success if you only talk about hair care on your website. No matter where the advertisement is placed on your blog, the content would be applicable.

Another benefit of creating a niche topic is expertise. You may be questioning a niche website because larger websites have plenty of sections and lots of different content, such as Daily Glow and even Elle.com. However, such sites can afford to hire writers to create hundreds of articles per month and have such high numbers in traffic that they are using other advertising programs that are much more targeted than Google Adsense. These websites may have agreements with other businesses for exclusive ad campaigns. If you are just starting out with no readers coming to your website, you need to think about establishing yourself as an expert. Why should readers choose your website compared to a reputable one, like Elle.com and Daily Glow? You need to think about becoming an expert in a single topic, so you can cover all content within that topic, including all news stories and product releases.

Speaking of topics and content creation, you need to make sure you are capable of keeping up with daily news, product releases and general content about your topic each week. If people are coming to your website for information on your chosen topic, such as hair care or cosmetics, they are expecting to see the latest news. You have to think about how much time you are devoting to the website and the content when you pick your niche. Sometimes, you need to evaluate how passionate you are about your chosen topic and how big of a demand there is.

It may take some time for you to find your niche, now that you see how beneficial it is for you to have one major topic rather than five smaller topic areas on your blog. Here are some things you need to consider when picking your niche.

- Think about the advertising possibilities: If you were to go out to smaller stores and target business owners in hopes of pitching an advertising package, what topic do you think would be more successful? Do you think you can easily pitch a campaign for a hair care product compared to a website covering all beauty topics? It may be more appealing for a business owner to go with the targeted content
- Topic development: While you may be passionate about one specific topic, you need to be able to think of topics for many weeks and months to come. Coming up with a couple won't be sufficient. You need to write a list of at least 20 to 50 article titles with more in mind to have a strong blog. While you don't have to know all of your blog titles in advance at all times, you should pick a topic you know

lots about and can continue to grow with over the years. Don't just pick something because you think it will make good money. You have to be passionate about it because you have to write about it for years to come

- Online magazine: If you want to have a magazine-style blog, you can create sub-categories for your beauty blog. For example, have categories such as "best cosmetics on the market," "cosmetics tutorials," "cosmetics reviews," and "cosmetics in the news." It would still be niche, but you can offer several things within the cosmetics industry

You may be finding yourself jotting down some ideas now for your beauty blog and I don't blame you. There is so much to do and so many directions you could take your beauty ideas. However, nothing can get done until you have a website. If you don't have a niche in mind, keep the pen and paper close by. You may just get inspired by the time we wrap up this chapter.

To start your website, there are a few things you need to do. If you have no experience creating a website, you need to know a few things. For one, you must understand what hosting is. Hosting is the place where your content is stored. For example, your articles, your pictures and your website aren't just floating around in the air. It has to be located somewhere to function. I can't give you a hosting company that you will like the most, but I can tell you that I use Blue Host and I can give you advice on how to set it up. If you choose to set up hosting with another company, the setup process may be similar. Some companies will offer services and help, meaning representatives will chat with you while you are setting up your account. Spend some time to do some research to see what services and prices will work for you.

Hosting isn't free. No matter what service you choose, you will have to pay something every month or once per year to host your website. You will have to pay for one year when you sign up. I can't tell you the prices since they may change often, but I can give you an idea; your hosting may cost $80 per year. Since you are registering your website, you are buying a domain as well which is about $20 per year ($10 for the domain and $10 for the security for the domain to protect your site). In other words, for one hosting account and one domain, you will be paying around $100 per year. If you don't have much money, it may seem like a lot. However, as a business expense, it is about as cheap as you can get. The best part is that the hosting fee doesn't change if you add another website, at least with Blue Host. Every website on top of that is just the $20 fee for a domain and the protection, meaning you can host five websites on your one hosting account for about $180 per year.

Hopefully by now you have some idea of what direction you want to take your blog. You have to think of a domain name for your blog. You want it to be focused and relevant to what you are blogging about. Avoid choosing something generic, such as beautyworld.com. It may not capture the attention of people who are looking for your niche topic. You cannot register your website with your hosting until you have a domain. You will get the option of checking to see if it is available on various extensions, including .com, .net and .org. Since Blue Host is U.S. based, the .ca extension is not available. For the best search results, you want to go for the .com extension, since companies often look for the .com extension. In case you ever get an offer to sell the blog to a bigger company, having the .com version will be a big influence on how much you can sell it for. In addition, people who are finding your website by typing in the domain name in the URL address bar will often use the .com extension by default.  The .com extension is very powerful and very valuable.

I will now go through what you will see if you are using Blue Host. I will show you every step from registration to finished site. The hosting account may appear overwhelming at first, because it has so many features, names and categories that you don't really need right away. In fact, many of the features you won't ever really need. If you want, you can always go back later and explore the options that your hosting service offers. Some features may be beneficial when your beauty blog grows.

*This is the menu of your Blue Host account as of October 2013. It provides you with everything you need to build your website and more. You can even register your domain through your C-Panel and attach your purchased domain to your hosting account.*

When you first log into the account after registering with your email, you will see the menu above. As part of your registration, you are providing your billing address and your payment information, meaning you can start purchasing domains immediately. This is a screen shot from the summer of 2013 after Blue Host did a design upgrade. Although it may be hard to see from the screenshot, you only really need the C-Panel option, which is the first big box in the picture. It is under the C-Panel that you handle everything from setting up the website to connecting your hosting account with Wordpress.

Under the C-Panel menu, you will see several options, including "Mail," "Site Builders" which will feature Wordpress, "Files," "Domains," "Upgrades," "Promotional," "Statistics," "Security, "Databases," "Software/ Services," "Preferences," "Advanced" and "Partners." You should be worried about the "Domains" section when you are getting started. Under the "Domains" section, you have several options.

*When you are starting out with your first domain, you need to register it to make your website. Without your website and theme, there is nothing for you to store or "host." Your "Domain Manager" option allows you to manage all of your websites. It is under the domains registration that you can choose from different extensions as well.*

Click on "Register Domain" under the "Domains" section of the C-Panel to register the domain you have chosen. I have gone through the process to show you how simple it is to get your domain registered and ready for your website.

*The screenshot above shows you what you will see once you click on "Register Domain" under the "Domains" menu. I have tried to see if www.beautyworld.com is available for the sake of this book. If you have something creative in mind, plug it into the space available and chose the .com extension. Click "check" to see if it is available.*

If you find that your chosen domain is not available, you have a few options. Of course, you could choose to buy the domain with a different extension, but you would be taken more seriously if you have the .com extension. You could try out different things, such as thebeautyworld.com instead of just beautyworld.com. Just because the domain isn't available doesn't mean you have to give up completely and change your niche. If you have a really good name, you don't have to give it up completely.

Choose a domain: `beautyworld`   `.com ▼`

`Check`

| Standard Domains* | .com ~~14.99~~ 11.99 | .org ~~14.99~~ 8.99 | .net ~~14.99~~ 9.99 | .us ~~14.99~~ 11.99 | .info ~~14.99~~ 11.99 | .biz ~~14.99~~ 11.99 | .cc ~~29.99~~ 24.99 | .tv ~~29.99~~ 24.99 |
|---|---|---|---|---|---|---|---|---|
| beautyworld | | | | | | | ☐ | ☐ |
| Beauty-Online | | ☐ | | ☐ | | | ☐ | ☐ |
| BeautyWorldCup | ☐ | ☐ | ☐ | ☐ | | ☐ | ☐ | ☐ |
| BeautyGroup | | ☐ | | ☐ | | | ☐ | ☐ |
| TheBeautyWorld | | ☐ | ☐ | ☐ | | | ☐ | ☐ |
| BeautyWorldTravel | ☐ | ☐ | ☐ | ☐ | | ☐ | ☐ | ☐ |
| BeautyWorldClass | | ☐ | ☐ | ☐ | | ☐ | ☐ | ☐ |
| BeautyWorldSeries | ☐ | ☐ | ☐ | ☐ | | ☐ | ☐ | ☐ |
| BeautyWorldOnline | | ☐ | ☐ | ☐ | | ☐ | ☐ | ☐ |
| BeautyWorldNews | | ☐ | ☐ | ☐ | | ☐ | ☐ | ☐ |

Show more suggestions...

*This is what you will be presented with when you try to find an available domain name. Your chosen domain name will be at the top of the list and other options are listed underneath. The test domain, "beautyworld.com" is not available for registration in this case.*

Once you find a domain that is available, click on the domain you wish to register and follow the directions. You will just have to confirm your purchase and credit card information unless you have saved the information to your account. Now, you have the hosting and you have the domain – now you need to connect the domain to a website you can design and you need to make sure it is all linked up to your hosting account.

Since your domain was registered through your Blue Host account, you don't need to worry about connecting your domain name with your hosting account. The two connected when you registered your domain through Blue Host. But you do need to worry about connecting your website platform (Wordpress) to your domain. Luckily, Blue Host has created an installation feature that allows you to connect a Wordpress platform with your hosting account and domain name.

To get started, go back to the C-Panel after your domain registration and scroll down until you see the "Site Builders" section. Click on the Wordpress icon. If you don't see the installation option immediately, scroll down to the "Script List" and find Wordpress under the "Blog" section. You want to click on the link that is beside the official blue Wordpress logo.

*You should see this installation option or something similar. Click on the Install option. You will then be presented with a page, where you can select the domain you want to install. Since you have only bought one domain, you should only have one option available. Click the legal agreement box and install the Wordpress platform for your website. When this process is complete, your website will be connected to both the hosting account and the domain name. You will have to repeat these steps for each domain you purchase in the future.*

Once you are done with the installation, you should check the email you have used to register your Blue Host account as the next step will be sent to your email. You will be sent some login information for your Wordpress platform. This platform is the one you will use from now on when you need to make changes to your website. The email you get will give you a password and a user name, which is either "admin" or your email.

To access your website, you need to go to your website with an extended "**/wp-admin**." For example, you need to visit www.thebeautyworld.com**/wp-admin**. This admin extension allows you to access your behind-the-scenes tools for your website so you can get started. You will probably find that you spend more time on the wp-admin panel than on your actual website once you start adding content and perfecting your site.

*This is the common appearance of your website's login page once you visit the /wp-admin page. "Admin" represents you as the website owner and the password required is in the registration e-mail. You may also be able to log in using your email address. Check the domain to ensure this is the right login page for your new website. You can change the password once you log in.*

You will see the Wordpress dashboard once you log in. You will see a menu panel down the left-hand side. Here you have plenty of options, including creating pages, creating posts, and installing plugins. However, you need to change your password first so you can remember your password in the future. The passwords provided by Wordpress are not easily remembered. Click on the "Users" option in the vertical left-hand-side panel. Make sure you choose the "Your Profile" option and then scroll down to the bottom. Right above the "Wordpress SEO Settings," you will see the password option.

Type in your new password twice and click save. You will be able to see how strong your password by checking the "Strength Indicator." If it is not strong enough, you can use upper and lower case letters and add symbols.

*This is exactly what it should look like when you are trying to set up your password. As you can see, you have the option of adding users, meaning you can register additional users under your account if you wanted to hire writers for your blog.*

Now that you have changed your password, you can start designing your website. When you register your website, you are given the standard template for Wordpress. Each year, they will issue a new free template that you can use to design your website. However, you can buy another themed template to really give your website that professional look.

# 1.2 Installing a Theme

For Wordpress themes, there is one place where you can find the most templates for your website – **themeforest.net**. There are other websites as well, but Theme Forest allows you to communicate with developers in case there is a file glitch with your purchased theme. You will even be able to find some that are simple enough to be used for a beauty website. If you are planning on sharing lots of content, including reviews or how-to tutorials, you may want to look for a simple theme, perhaps with a black and white color scheme. Most themes are customizable.

Many of the themes will allow you to change colors and backgrounds, so just because you don't like what you see during the preview of the theme doesn't mean it won't work for your blog. You need to look at the layout and functionality, as details can be changed. Read through the descriptions of the theme to make sure you have full creative control.

You have thousands of themes to choose from and many of them fall under $50. The more detailed or extensive templates could cost you a little more, but you don't necessarily need to purchase a theme more than $50. The themes available for this price will give you everything you need and more to really personalize your beauty blog.

If you have any questions in regards to the theme, you can go to the theme's page or the author's personal page under the themeforest.net site to see how others have rated the theme. You will also be able to see how many people have purchased the theme before you, how many comments people have left in regards to the theme and learn more about the compatibilities of the theme. For example, you can learn about the theme's compatible browsers, whether the theme has high resolution, what files you will get when you purchase it (CSS Files, JS Files, PHP Files, for example – these will all help you in the customization of the site), and whether you can add those free plugins I discussed earlier.

I would suggest you browse through themeforest.net before making a final purchase. There are hundreds of themes available and most of them may suit your needs. Search different options to see what you like the best.

This is one example of a theme you can download. This is the "Sahifa" theme from TieLabs and is available through Themeforest.net. This theme will give you a featured news slider with social media icons.

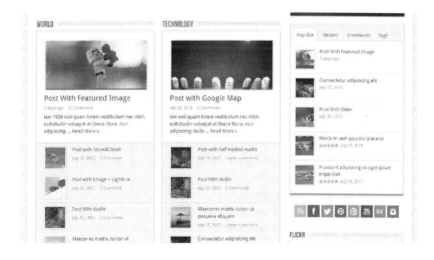

This is the same theme just further down the home page. It gives you plenty of options to have lots of beauty tutorials and articles on the front page. Keep in mind that you can change the colors and backgrounds to make it suit your blogging vision or brand.

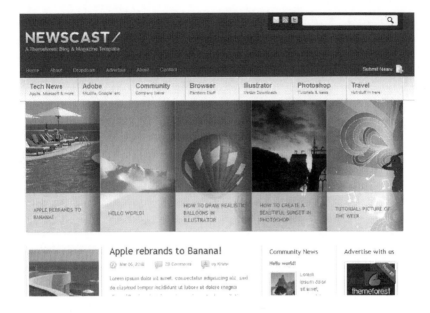

This is another theme which you can use for your blog. This gives a more interactive feel because of the accordion slider. This theme is called "News Cast" by Kriesi.

This is what the theme looks like on the front page. Again you have plenty of options when it comes to personal customization. This theme gives you plenty of content on the home page.

You can also go for a simpler theme that allows your pictures and content to stand out more. One such theme is "Showycase" by Premitheme. This is more like a portfolio and photography theme, which is great if you can go to local events in your community and get those stories yourself.

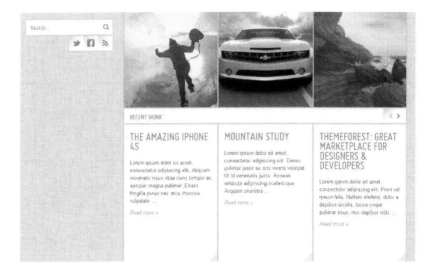

This is what the theme looks like on the front page. Your pictures will stand out with a brief description, which is a teaser to the article.

At first glance, these themes may not be what you had envisioned for your beauty blog. You may be envisioning a softer background, more natural shades of pink and oranges and perhaps going for a warmer feel. You shouldn't judge the themes on these particulars because the themes are often customizable. Instead, judge the themes on the amount of pictures and content on the home page or the types of sliders or presentation features they offer as these features are the ones you are buying.

Once you have made a decision to purchase your theme, you need to purchase it through Themeforest.net. You can choose to buy it via your credit card or use your PayPal account to make the purchase. You will be able to download the theme immediately. It will be downloaded in a zip file, so save the files to your desktop. You may have to go into your "downloads" section of your themeforest.net profile to access the zip folder if it doesn't download automatically. With the download, you will be given a documentation file, which explains how to set up the theme and give you useful information about formatting the theme to make it your own.

To install the theme, locate "Appearances" in the left-hand menu of your Wordpress panel. Under here, you will find the "Themes" option. Click on this and choose the "Install Themes" tab underneath the page's title. Select the "Upload" option to locate your downloaded zipped folder theme on your computer and wait until it uploads and installs. You are now installing your purchased theme with your website and domain.

If you have troubles uploading your newly purchased theme to your websites, it could have something to do with the way the developer has packaged the theme. The developer may have put the zipped folder containing the theme into another zipped folder with all of the documentation you need to learn how to use the folder. The documentation won't install as a theme and hence the installation will fail. If this is the case, locate the zipped folder and open it up. If there is another zipped folder with the same name as the theme itself within the original zipped folder, then drag this zipped folder out of the original and place it on your computer desktop. Try installing the theme now with the folder you have dragged onto your desktop and wait to see what happens. Refresh the website to see if the theme has worked. The new theme should appear on your website. It will look rather plain, but you are getting a fresh canvas to work with.

# 1.3 Personalizing Your Website

Now that you have uploaded your theme, you can start designing your website to make it uniquely your own. You may already have an idea of what color scheme you want to use or have an idea of how you want the layout to be based on the theme you bought. This is your chance to make the site targeted towards beauty readers. Some themes won't look like much when you first upload them because they are canvases for users.

*This is an example of a design panel that a theme may have to help you design your website. This is a panel offered by Pexeto, a theme creator I use for a couple of my websites. This panel provides you with options to customize every background, picture and link.*

You may have an idea in mind to make it black, white and pink, or perhaps even a coral color scheme to make it softer. Each theme will have some kind of panel that allows you to make the theme your own in terms of colors, unless you buy one that is uniquely designed to be purely black and white. You can usually determine this by the previews Theme Forest offer. If you do choose a theme with customization options, this type of panel shown on the previous page will automatically install into your Wordpress panel once you install the theme.

Since you are running a blog and have potential plans of growing it into a larger business or brand, you should also do a copyright statement for your website. Some themes will allow you to incorporate a copyright statement in footer of the theme manually. If not, you have to go into the "Editor" section and find the "Footer" HTML code. In here, you should find a line that has the words "Copyright" and the name of the theme creator. You can take out the name of the theme creator and change the name to your own blog or magazine name.

*This is an example of a very detailed copyright statement that you will find at the bottom of your website. This particular sample is from Cosmopolitan.com. You can simple write "Copyright 2013 – name of your website. All Rights Reserved." Privacy Policy and Terms of Use can be placed under your menu or "About" page in the footer menu.*

Now that you have a copyright statement and the colors picked out, you should install a plugin that will help your ranking in search engines. As described earlier in this book, your ranking is very powerful. Not only does it help you with exposure, but it can also make you more money. There is one plugin that can help you get into search engines rather quickly. This plugin is called YOAST SEO plugin and it allows you to control your major keywords, your page descriptions, your meta-description and your overall presence in search engines. This is how it looks.

| | |
|---|---|
| Site keywords | |
| Home Page Description | |
| Home page title | |
| Page title separator | |

*This is from the Pexeto theme as well and allows you to customize your title and your website's meta-description.*

### Daily Glow: Skin Care, Hair Care, and Beauty Tips
www.dailyglow.com/ ▾
Do you want to glow from the inside out? Get the latest on healthy beauty: skin care, hair care, beauty tips and hygiene tips at Daily Glow.

*This is what Daily Glow's website looks like in a Google search. The homepage title is "Daily Glow: Skin Care, Hair Care and Beauty Tips." The keyword is "Daily Glow," as it appears in the website title, the domain and the meta-description. The meta-description, also known as the homepage description, is the section starting with, "Do you want to glow from the inside out?" By using the YOAST plugin, you have control over this crucial information.*

Once you have taken care of the design, your copyright issues and your SEO information for your website, you can start creating those static pages. Static pages are those that never change, no matter how much content you add over time. Examples include "about," "contact," "contributors," "terms of use" and "privacy policy." If you are planning on running a blog with multiple writers down the line, you can also outline contribution requirements. An example of a menu is below. Keep in mind that each of these pages should be have their respective YOAST SEO information. You will have a section to do so on each page and post you publish.

| Skin & Beauty | Hair Care | Personal Care | Makeover | Beauty News | Experts | Product Reviews |
| --- | --- | --- | --- | --- | --- | --- |

*This is an example of a static menu. It can be on the top of the page or the bottom. Some themes will allow menus on both the top and the bottom, but it is up to you to decide what works best for your website layout. It is wise to put desirable topics across the top of the blog, and put informational links in the bottom menu, such as "about," "contact," and "privacy policy." Topics from this menu sample would be more desired by your readers.*

Now that you have a menu in place, your website may be taking some shape, but it may still look dull because of the lack of content. Many say that the front page of a blog should function as a magazine cover – you want to offer a little bit of everything. People also refer to the homepage as a point of reference. In other words, you will need to put all of your latest news on the homepage.

You do this by changing the template of the homepage. It may be set as the default template when you install the theme, but you should change it to feature the latest news. You do this by clicking on the pages, creating a home page, and setting the home page to the "featured" page under "template" in the publishing option. You may have to go under "Settings" and then "Reading" to change the "Front Page Display" to "Static Page" and then "Home." The documentation for the theme should be of help.

*Right under the publishing panel, you will see this. Under the "Template" option, you can set it to "Featured page" to get all of your new blogs on the home page. This drop-down menu is part of the publishing area of the pages section. You can examine what each layout looks like on Theme Forest under the preview section of the theme.*

You may quickly discover that you have options when it comes to your page layout. You can have a "full width" page, where your written content will go from one side to the other. This is not something you often see on content sites, because sidebars are valuable for advertisements and additional content. These sidebars can be placed on either side. They can be customized, so you can feature the content you want to share, which could include product reviews, ads or even relevant articles.

You can also download plugins so you can really customize your sidebars, including a Twitter feed, a social media icon plugin and you can implement HTML code in the text box, so you can feature pictures with embedded links. You customize the sidebars under the "Widgets" section of the Wordpress panel, where you can create several different sidebars for pages and posts. You can create as many sidebars as you want for your blog, which may spark further reading by your visitors.

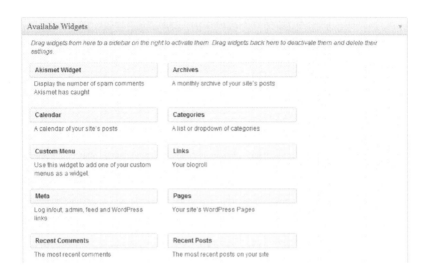

These are some of the custom widgets that come with the Wordpress theme. You can share your blog post archives so readers can sort your posts by month and year. There is also a calendar option, a categories section if you arrange your posts by categories, a recent comments option and a recent posts option. You don't have to use them if you don't find them appropriate for your website.

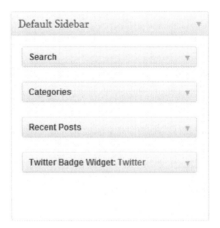

This "Default Sidebar" sample is right next to the "Available Plugins" section of the "Widgets" section. You simply drag the plugins you want in your sidebar into the default sidebar. Here, you can see a sidebar with a search bar, categories, recent posts and Twitter.

You have now created your website with your chosen theme. You have also customized the website with a copyright statement, a meta-description and learned how to make your sidebars and pages stand out. You can now start adding your first couple of articles to see how your articles and the featured images for each article will show up on your blog. You may find that some things need to be readjusted, but you can only do that with some content on the site. Perhaps you like the sidebar more on the left than on the right after the content is added.

*This is an example of how a website looks when the sidebar is active. This is from my old personal blogging website and you can see how the social media icons, my search bar option and my Twitter feed is in a sidebar, completely separated from my blogging content. In this example, the sidebar is on the right-hand side, but you can quickly change it to be on the left-hand side if you wish. You do this under the page in question by scrolling down to the sidebar section of the page.*

As you start adding content, you have to become more consistent in your online behaviour. As soon as people start finding your content, they will be expecting more content frequently. If you only have a few days a week to write, make sure you keep on schedule on those days. If you publish 10 articles one day and nothing the following two weeks, you are giving readers no reason to return. It is much better to space them out and lure people in slowly each day.

Your blog may look a little dull with just a few articles, but that will quickly fill up if you have plenty of ideas. While you want to add enough content to fill up your home page, you should keep adding content on a consistent basis. Your readers will be expecting new content and if you let them down, they may find another reliable blog to read. It is so easy to lose readers, so don't give them a reason to leave your blog.

If you feel very motivated one day but know that things won't be as relaxed in the upcoming weeks, you can schedule your content. If you have written 20 articles, you can space them out in terms of publishing. You don't even have to be at the computer when each post is published. The Wordpress platform allows you to schedule your work in advance, meaning you can plan out your posts for quite some time. That way, you can take advantage of your creativity one day and give your readers spaced out content. This is called "automating posts." While you may not use this feature on a regular basis, you should use it if you plan on going out of town for vacation or just need to have a few days with no work. Your readers will be expecting to read your news, so you can schedule work ahead of time, so your readers are not affected.

Scheduling your post is a neat feature if you know that you won't have time to publish anything for the weeks to come. Chances are that you will find the tool useful on more than one occasion. While it is tempting to schedule your posts and then take a week off, I highly suggest you only schedule posts in advance if you know that you will be prevented from doing so. You want to be available if news breaks, so you don't write about the event days later. Readers have high expectations, so don't leave them hanging unless it is absolutely necessary.

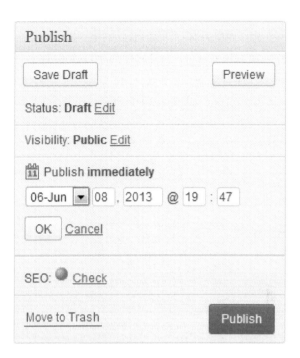

*This is how you automate your posts. In the publishing frame of your post section, you will see a publishing time. It will say "immediately." If you click "edit," you will be able to change the date and the time that the post will publish. You can do this to any post you are planning on publishing at a later date.*

Once you have created your website and start adding some content, you may notice that your logo and your website name is missing from the top of your website. Even though it is super simple to upload a logo in Wordpress, you should do so with some thought. I have saved this section until now because branding is becoming such a big part of online blogging and internet businesses.

Many themes will make room for a logo and a website name, because logo recognition is such an integral part of website branding. Many of the bigger beauty websites don't actually have a logo – they just use the name of the website and company as the logo itself. Some may have a small logo, such as the Daily Glow circle, but it is rare. In other words, the name of the website is a big part of the brand itself, so it would be totally acceptable if you wanted to skip out on a logo.

In the next couple of sub-chapters, I will try to explain what a brand is and how you should start developing your own web brand from the first day. You should play around with some lettering and logo design and then be very consistent in using it on all of your business cards, website pages and social media profiles once you decide on a logo or design.

# 1.4 What's in a Brand?

Branding is a very complex thing. It is about how people feel about something and how something evokes emotions. The idea of a brand is not something tangible. You can't brand something overnight. It is a trust that it built and generated over time. There have been many discussions as to what a brand really is. A brand is something that describes the entire business or website as a whole – something that connects the goal of the business with the desire of the readers. It really comes down to a connection that brings readers back to the website instead of going elsewhere.

In other words, the brand is something specific that the website gives to the readers. The name, the logo, the slogan and the design can all contribute to the brand. And branding can also come down to trust for something like a beauty blog. Offering tutorials or product reviews could either convince someone to trust your information or find the same information on another site. Branding is about building trusting relationships with readers.

There are many ways you can design your logo or website name, but your niche and vision will ultimately play a role. While you may just want to stick with the website name as your logo, you should make it stand out, so don't use common fonts that can easily be copied or used by other websites similar to your own. Below, I have provided three examples of how bigger fashion and beauty websites have used their names as the brand rather than a logo in rather simplistic ways from my second book.

# GLAMOUR

This is the "Glamour" logo from the official website. It is bold, fuchsia and large. Because it is all capital letters, it does set itself up as an authoritative source for all things glamour and fashion. This is one example of how branding can be in the name rather than a logo.

GAMES / PROMOTIONS / FREE STUFF / NEWSLETTER

# COSMOPOLITAN

| HION | DIET/FITNESS | FOOD/COCKTAILS | CAREER/MONEY | COSMO F |
|------|--------------|----------------|--------------|---------|

"Cosmopolitan" is another example of how lettering can make the logo and branding stand out. It is similar to the "Glamour" logo, except that the pink color is a bit different. The letters are closer together and made thinner. It could resemble the big skyscrapers of New York City. This logo is also from the official website.

dailyglow where health meets beauty

| | Skin & Beauty | Hair Care | Personal Care | Mal |
|---|---------------|-----------|---------------|-----|

"Daily Glow" is a rather new website that deals primarily with beauty regimes and products. However, "Daily Glow" combines a little logo within the website name to make it truly unique on the website. The "O" in "glow" stands out. Whenever that specialized "O" is present, readers know that it is related to "Daily Glow." This logo is on all of the social media pages related to the site for branding purposes.

You don't have to use the name of the website as your primary logo. You can get creative and develop something along the lines of "Daily Glow" where the logo is part of the name. You can also have a separate logo that stands out, so your blog name becomes secondary. You can also integrate the website' colors into your logo, as "Daily Glow" has done with dark grey, light grey and pink. Your logo is something that should represent you and your blog, so you know it best. Just make sure it makes an impression.

If you don't have any experience with logo designs, there are plenty of sources available to help you out. One of these online resources is Vistaprint.ca, which helps small business owners develop logos and business merchandise for low prices. You can purchase a logo package for about $22, which will give you everything you need to get started on your website. They have hundreds of logos available. If you don't like any of them, you could perhaps get some inspiration as to what your logo could be.

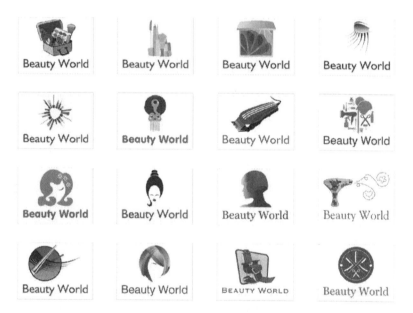

*This is an example of the logos that are available for beauty and health-related businesses. If you are doing a niche blog on make tutorials or hair care, you may find one of these logos useful. If not, you can always see what you like and perhaps get some inspiration.*

You should take your time in coming up with a logo, as you are creating a powerful brand. By the time you have created your website, chosen your color scheme, added some content to your website and added some sidebars, your logo may come organically. You may already know what direction you want to take. If you change your mind, make sure you change it before you get too many readers. You can imagine the confusion if Elle.com or even a large beauty and fashion magazine decided to change the logo around to something new.

Your logo is very powerful, whether you are using an icon, a name or a combination of both. You will start using it on everything, including your social media profiles, your business cards and on every webpage and blog post you create on your website. In other words, your logo will be everywhere. It is something that people will recognize instantly when browsing through articles online or searching for content on social media networks.

Because the brand and logo carry so much weight for your beauty blog, you have to protect it. If you start analyzing some of the bigger fashion magazines or blogs, you will see that they are meticulously about everything they post, whether it is an article or a tweet on Twitter about the newest summer trends. Everything has a goal and everything can be linked back to the blog or brand in question. For example, you don't see a large fashion brand posting about the stock market news, or see an editor sharing what she had for dinner last night on the company's Twitter feed. Everything that is done in the name of the brand is done to protect the brand's goals, message and perception. Many brands represent something much bigger. And even though you are creating a website alone, you should align yourself with these big websites. Chances are you will find success if you are professional.

These larger websites also understand who they are and what message they are sending. Perhaps you need a direction before creating your logo. Do you want to be the top beauty product review site online? Or do you want to offer the largest collection of eye-makeup tutorials in video format? Perhaps, you find it more appealing to sell yourself as a cosmetics lover who will take the e-commerce approach to sell products in an affiliate format. Don't feel discouraged if you don't have an identity within minutes. It could take months or even years to really establish that identity. Just understand your goals and your direction and everything else should fall into place.

# Chapter 2:
# Finding Content

If you have read my book, "How to Become a Fashion Writer: Taking Your Writing to the Runway," you may have found the first chapter a bit redundant. Setting up a website is the same procedure, whether you are focusing on beauty or fashion blogging – or any other topic for that matter. But the rest of this book is directly applicable to beauty blogging. And this chapter is all about the articles and content you will be sharing on your beauty blog.

As your website is starting to take shape, you may find yourself on the prowl looking for more content to share. This chapter will be devoted to tackling the troubles of using pre-written content and how you can write opinion pieces based on news articles without being penalized in search engines. As you may find during the first couple of months of writing, blogging is all about a specific cycle; you write content, you share content, you continue to share content and you hope for clicks to make some money. Then you write some new content and you hope that this new article will make you a few dollars here and there.

In other words, much of your time will be spent on finding new topics for your blog and crafting these articles. And if you are writing beauty news, such as covering the red carpet at a major event from home, you may be keeping busy. However, you may be struggling to find content on days where there isn't much happening on red carpets around the world. Social media is making it easier for blogs and websites to get information for stories directly from companies and celebrities. For example, a big celebrity may post a picture of herself on her personal Twitter or Instagram account before attending an event or hitting the red carpet. And that content is a great chance for you to cover this celebrity's look for the event, including everything from makeup to hair.

Many celebrity writers are using basic tweets to create articles for gossip sites, because the information sent out from social media accounts is often coming directly from the celebrities themselves. They no longer have to issue press releases or set up interviews to get information out to readers. And beauty bloggers can use the same type of procedure to get content.

If you look at larger websites such as Elle.com or any gossip website, you will see that they publish several stories per day. If you want to make a career out of blogging, you need to be continuously publishing content to keep readers coming back. However, if you are just starting out with this blogging venture, you may not have any idea as to where to find your content. I have a few suggestions that I will share with you here, but you can be creative as long as you don't steal content from other sites.

As a beauty writer, you will have to find beauty content related to your niche. This could include new product releases or big celebrity events, for example. You could choose to work hard on your blog yourself, or choose to hire writers and put the pressure on them to find the content. There are pros and cons to both methods and you choose your own direction based on what motivates you. This is your blog and you have to keep yourself loving this beauty blog for months and years to come.

- **Product Reviews**: As you start crafting your articles, you should focus on bringing out the best in beauty, whether you are giving a tutorial or offering a review. While you want to share your opinions on the products or services, you want to think about your future relationships with the product developers or companies. If you don't like using a certain hair color product, don't criticize the entire company, for example. Of course, you want to offer honest reviews and articles, but you want to be professional as well. Don't just focus on the positive products, but avoid being too harsh when a product doesn't satisfy. There are plenty of negative people in the world that will have something to say about products they don't like. You need to think about your reputation and your professionalism

Of course, you don't have to focus on product reviews if you want to offer how-to articles. There are two ways you can go; you can incorporate product reviews as part of your blogging focus if your niche is eye makeup, for example. Another direction is focusing solely on product reviews and incorporating many products. This way, you become the expert that people go to if they are trying to get information on specific products.

You may be looking for a new direction for your content if you find yourself stuck in a rut. One way to get some new content onto your blog is to get some guest bloggers to share some content, so you get some fresh perspective on the site.

- **Guest Bloggers**: If you want another opinion on your website, you can offer a post for guest-writer who wants to share his or her experiences or reviews of beauty products. While some bloggers will demand a fee for an article, others will do it for free if they can get some exposure on your website and get experience for their resumes. If you do choose to get a guest blogger for your blog or a guest contributor, make sure you create a contract for the guests to protect yourself. The content they write for you should belong to you exclusively. I will touch upon this more later, but you should know that this is an option

Another benefit of having guest bloggers on board once in a while is the readership that comes with these bloggers. For example, you may have one or two guest bloggers who each have a respective readership of 3000 to 5000 readers. When these bloggers share their presence on your blog, your personal readership could grow. A growing readership is important because you can make more money.

- **Growing Readership**: Your readership may grow once you start sharing more and more content. And you should be keeping up with your traffic numbers via Google Analytics. You need to set this up during the early stages of your website setup. You can use these numbers to pitch to advertisers, as a company may be willing to invest in an advertising campaign on your website, if you can prove that your website about hair, for example, gets at least 30,000 views per month. Of course, it can be difficult to get readers to your website. Even though you may feel a little discouraged in the beginning when you are getting less than 100 views per month, you should focus on the big picture. The more you write the more exposure you may get.

Now that you have a brief introduction to the various directions you can take your blog, let's look at three methods that could help define your brand. First, I'll talk about getting inspiration from other websites when it comes to articles and written content. Then, I'll talk about being the trusted product reviewer. Finally, I'll touch upon getting the beauty news when it hits the web. You can choose one or combine all three methods on your blog. The most important thing about choosing one or more directions is to remember your niche and how your readers will react to your blog.

- Example 1: A hair blog that has both product reviews about hair care products, as well as written tutorials
- Example 2: A makeup blog that focuses on written tutorials and a news section that introduces new makeup products on the market
- Example 3: A product review blog that combines all beauty products

# 2.1 Get Inspired By Other Websites

As I mentioned in the previous sub-chapter, you can use other websites to get inspired for articles and content. Many websites do this online and the key is to be original, even though many websites are reporting on the same story. For example, one celebrity may have a wardrobe malfunction on the red carpet and one tabloid may publish the story first. Within hours, the story has spread on the internet as other tabloids and blogs pick up on the story. The reason why they all index in Google and Google News is because they have original reporting. In other words, none of the top ranking websites in search engines have copied or scraped articles. Quotes cannot be altered, but everything else should be original reporting.

This is the same type of mind frame you need to have if you will be using other websites' content for your own blog. You need to reference the website if you take the quotes by linking to it through your own article on the blog. You can do a simple Google search to find these articles. Or you can set up an account with Google Alerts. Google Alerts inform you every time someone publishes something online in regards to specific topics. You can choose the keywords you want to be informed about. Examples include "beauty," "beauty tutorials," "hair tutorials," "face treatments," and so forth. You can choose keywords that fit your niche rather than cover everything in the industry. As soon as something is published online, you will get an email with all of the appropriate links so you can get started on your work.

As mentioned above, there are some rules that come with "borrowing" a news story for your own website. Many bloggers will take the main meat from the story, such as direct quotes from a celebrity or stylist, and add their personal commentary. Writers will change the title of the content in hopes of catching the attention of readers while adding their own perspective or commentary to the story. I've provided an example on the next page of how several websites report on the same story.

Newlywed **Zoe Saldana** brings the glamour to the **red carpet** in yet ...

Daily Mail - 10 hours ago

She got married in secret five months ago, but **Zoe Saldana** ... The Avatar star looked elegant and stylish as she hit the **red carpet** for the 7th ...

Zoe Saldana & Amy Adams: Hamilton Behind The Camera Awards ...

Just Jared - 7 hours ago

Jeremy Renner, **Zoe Saldana**, Joe Manganiello & More Get Glam ...

Socialite Life - 3 hours ago

all 4 news sources »

**Zoe Saldana's** Look Is Side-Splitting — But Not In A Ha-Ha Way

Refinery29 - by Gina Marinelli - Nov 4, 2013

We've seen many an hourglass-faking dress before, yet the sneaky trick never seems to lose its magic. And, at the LACMA Art + Film Gala this ...

+ Show more

**Red Carpet: Zoe Saldana** Stuns In Illusion Dress Featuring Full ...

TheGloss - by Samantha Escobar - Nov 4, 2013

LOS ANGELES, CA – NOVEMBER 02: Actress **Zoe Saldana** arrives at the LACMA 2013 Art + Film Gala on November 2, 2013 in Los Angeles, ...

**Red carpet** review: Lily Collins, **Zoe Saldana** tangled up in blue

Los Angeles Times - by Booth Moore - Oct 31, 2013

Pantone announced "dazzling blue" as a *key color for 2014, fashion designers showed many hues of blue on the spring 2014 runways, and ...

*This is an example of a red carpet story. Zoe Saldana, a famous Hollywood actress, hit the red carpet in a stunning dark blue dress. The story was repeated on several websites, but as you can see, each website has a different title and an original article about the simple story.*

This story of Zoe Saldana on the red carpet at the LACMA 2013 Art and Film Gala is essentially just one story, but many blogs and websites pick it up. Even though a story may be exclusive to one website, the story will get rewritten by many websites over time. It is very much acceptable for you to get inspired by other websites, but don't copy the article. Add your own content and be very original on your blog. If possible, simply use the quotes and link back to the original article and mention the website by name. That way, you aren't stealing any content that isn't legally yours.

As you are writing the content, make sure that you are using the name of the person or product you are reporting on. If you are doing a tutorial, make sure you have the phrases "eye makeup tutorial" or "smoky eye tutorial" several times throughout the content, as these are the words people will be using to search for your content, for example. The general rule of thumb is to use the keywords near the beginning of the article and in the title, and then about every 300 -500 words throughout the article. More than that could result in your content being labelled spam, so use them sparingly.

# 2.2 Product Reviews

Beauty products are a huge part of the beauty industry. Many would argue that the beauty industry wouldn't be an industry on its own if it wasn't for the many products being sold daily around the globe. It therefore only makes sense that product reviews should be considered for any beauty blogger. Of course, you don't personally have to review all of the products yourself, as this may empty your wallet and stuff your bathroom closets with samples. However, you can use your blogging platform to provide a space for others to share their experiences with the products.

There are many benefits to letting others share their thoughts about certain products on your blog. For one, you have people sharing content and people reading content. That means more visits, which could mean more income from product advertisements. In addition, you are reviewing products on the blog, which means you could start selling these products on your site, adding another income stream. I will talk more about this in chapter 5, where I offer more advice for monetizing your blog. For now, just determine whether product review is a strategy you want to incorporate on your beauty blog.

The following two pages are some product review samples from Total Beauty, which is a beauty product review website (totalbeauty.com). This is to give you an idea of what product reviews could look like. If you do choose to work with product reviews, you should find a theme on Theme Forest that allows you to publish reviews, preferably with a ratings system.

*Jane Iredale PurePressed Base Mineral Foundation SPF 20*

 **9.1** See all 72 reviews

*MAC Studio Fix Powder Plus Foundation*

 **8.8** See all 191 reviews

*Amazing Cosmetics Velvet Mineral Powder*

 **9.3** See all 24 reviews

*Jane Iredale Amazing Base SPF 20*

 **9.4** See all 41 reviews

*This is an example of how beauty product reviews can be set up on a website platform. It is a simple look that showcases the product and has a clear rating from readers. People can also read the reviews in detail.*

# TIGI Catwalk Curlesque Curls Rock Amplifier

AS LOW AS $5.58  BUY NOW

**9.3**
TOTALBEAUTY.COM PRODUCT RATING

*39 reviews*
See the Breakdown

SEE ALL REVIEWS

Product Info | Add Your Review

———— *tigi catwalk curlesque curls rock amplifier* ————
*reviews*

## Coaxed perfect curls from my wavy hair

At first I thought the curls were a little too perfect. They formed these flawless little spirals all over my head and even though I was pleased with how shiny, full of body, and well-defined they were, I felt a bit too Shirley Temple. So I brushed them out and then rubbed a bit of pomade through the whole mass and was thrilled to see that the shape of the curls returned, only they looked much mor...**read more** — *4 years, 12 months ago*

teshie | 396 reviews
ALL-STAR

This review is: Helpful | Not helpful | Inappropriate | 9 of 12 people said helpful

## curls do indeed rock

I looovveee this product. I have been encountering hair issues lately. I'm not sure if it's my age, the weather, medication or what but the texture of my curls has changed dramatically. My hair is curly normally with a coarse texture, but since I went sulfate free, my curls have become much softer and nothing seems to hold them in place past an hour. I tried many different products and nothing...**read more** — *7 months, 2 weeks ago*

*This example is from the same website for a single product. You can see that individual people have the right to share their experiences on the website and give the product a rating. In other words, you are opening up the platform for others to share reviews – not just yours.*

You can choose to have people review products if they have something to say on your website, while you focus on writing content for your website. For example, people and readers may offer reviews for beauty products, while you yourself may write news releases for brand new products to the market or even offer some tutorials with some of the products you share. This gives you the power of your blog and the content. If you do choose to write the product reviews yourself, make sure you don't disregard other people's experiences with the product. For hair, people have different hair types and textures, which could change the effects of the products. For makeup, some products may not be suitable to people who have sensitive skin. You will always have people who share a different opinion from your own, so make sure your blog offers a more honest review, even though you personally don't agree. You never know what people are looking for.

# 2.3 Interviews

An interview is another way of getting original content onto your beauty blog. While product reviews will definitely give your beauty blog an original edge, you could get tons of new readers if you can land an interview with someone famous. One approach is to target companies or celebrities, who would be willing to share some beauty tips or perhaps product releases for your beauty blog.

However, people you interview do not have to be famous and sought out. In fact, some of the more powerful stories come from regular people with powerful stories. For example, one person may have the story that a company provided her with new products after she had a bad experience with a new product line. Or maybe someone had a scary experience with a product because of an unknown allergy. The possibilities are endless; as long as you make sure that your niche is in focus for these interviews. Here are two examples of other types of interviews you could keep in mind as your beauty blog grows.

**Lash primer:** We're all for voluminous lashes, but between your eyelash curler and your actual mascara, you're more than covered.

**Neck, foot and any body-part-specific cream:** We understand that the skin on your body varies in terms of dryness and sensitivity, but how different can all of these creams honestly be? We're going to go ahead and give you permission to use plain old body lotion everywhere except your face.

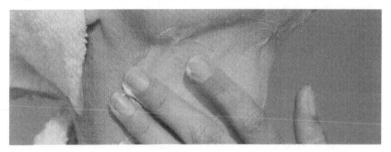

**Toner:** It's intended as an extra step between cleansing and moisturizing to help reduce the appearance of pores, but it mostly just makes our skin feel tight and dry (and we're not alone!). Plus, most people don't even know what toner is.

*This is an example of how an interview could look with readers. If you want to do a list of the best products or techniques for a single thing, such as makeup removal, you could create an interview-style article with tips and stories from regular users or your readers.*

Related Photo:

In our interview, Lilly reveals her diet and workout secrets and how she stays centered while juggling a busy work schedule and her newfound fame.

Question: What is your workout routine, and how often do you work out?

" First off, let me say that I am very lucky in that I am genetically blessed in this department. God gives us each something great — maybe beautiful eyes, great lips, gorgeous hair — whatever it may be, I definitely got skinny genes! Being naturally thin is a great help in staying fit, I know how much of a struggle it is for those that have to work twice as hard due to genetics, and I respect their hustle.

With that said, I do work out about three times a week. I am NOT a gym person, I can't just go to the gym and work out on my own. I need my workouts to be fun and stimulating.

*This is an example of a beauty interview that has been done with reality star, Lilly Ghalichi from "Shahs of Sunset." The interview focuses on her beauty regimes and her staying health by offering some tips and advice. This is another type of interview you can have on your beauty blog once in a while. Just keep it more beauty-focused, not health-focused.*

When you are just starting your blog, you may have troubles landing interviews with bigger names or companies. Famous entities will often donate time and energy to an interview if they see a marketing opportunity, especially if they are doing the interview for free. In other words, if you are only reaching between 100 and 5000 people per month, it may be hard to land an exclusive interview with someone famous.

However, you should never let that be the reason why you stop blogging about beauty. Chances are that *excluding* celebrities or famous people on your blog could make you stand out, *because* of that reason – targeting regular people. So many websites are aiming to make an impression with their connections, but people often want to read real stories from real people.

You can focus on getting inspiration from product reviews and content from other websites until you find you have enough readers and enough contacts to create an excellent interview about something interesting. You want to surprise your readers with something new in an interview – not give them something they can find on 16 other websites.

# Chapter 3: News vs. Evergreen Content

If you do a random search on blogs of any kind, you will find that they are split into three categories; general news, evergreen content and a mix of the two. For example, Us Weekly – also known as Us Magazine – combines traditional celebrity news with evergreen articles, such as "the best makeup tips for the red carpet." These two types of articles are combined on the website. While the news part is updated daily, the evergreen section is updated when necessary, such as during awards season. Then, you have websites that solely focus on news content, because they have access to Google News, a program that organizes the newest stories online. And finally, you have websites that focus on evergreen content. These are often called "content mills" because they generate articles for readers that are as applicable now as in five years. For example, an article titled "how to apply dark eye makeup" is just as applicable now as it is in five or ten years. Sure, there will be new beauty products, but the techniques used now may be highly relevant in the future as well.

Right now, you may have your niche picked out, but still debating as to which direction you want to take the beauty blog. You don't have to have all of the answers right now. But you should have an idea as to what content you want to share; do you want to be glued to the internet and report news, or do you want to offer more useful and in-depth information, such as how-to articles, product reviews or tutorials? The following chapter is all about distinguishing the two and how they can both be profitable.

# 3.1 News: Learning the Ropes of Beauty News

One way to learn how beauty news should be written is to read content from the major websites that share news – *and* gets included in Google News. Another way is to examine Google News and the requirements for getting content included in the program. Either way, you need to familiarize yourself with news content if you want to have beauty news, red carpet events and even some celebrity stories as part of your beauty blog. For Google and most search engines, "news content" is labelled as events that happened within the last 48 hours and events that will happen within the next seven days. For example, you can write about a red carpet event and cover all of the beauty looks if you do so within 48 hours of the event happening. In addition, you can write about an event about seven days in advance and it would be considered news. But if you do a comparison article between two beauty looks, both of which were red carpets event two weeks prior, it would not be considered news. It is important to know these rules if you want to get included in Google News.

**Google** beauty 🎤 🔍

Web    Images    Maps    News    More ▾    Search tools

About 215,000,000 results (0.24 seconds)

**Canada's First Fashion & Beauty Blogger Conference Ignites Its ...**
Canada NewsWire (press release) - 4 hours ago
11, 2013 /CNW/ - Spark Sessions, Canada's first fashion and **beauty** blogger conference, will premiere as the ultimate Canuck connection point ...

**'Beauty** and the Beast' scoop: Elisabeth Rohm scores guest arc as...
Entertainment Weekly - 4 hours ago
Elisabeth Rohm is going to bring a little law and order to **Beauty** and the Beast. EW has learned that the actress, best known for her role as ADA ...
+ Show more

*Google News is located in the main menu of Google, labelled "News." It is here you can find content that has been pre-approved by Google to be classified as news content. It takes effort to get included in Google News, but you will experience an increase in page views and get more exposure. With more page views comes the potential of more earnings.*

## News for **beauty news**

**How to replenish your make-up kit for winter**
Metro - 9 hours ago
Let's face it, the weather is changing and it's getting colder so it's about time we got into A/W **beauty** action. I want to draw attention to the fact ...

**New-age beauty:** Imelda Burke
New Zealand Herald - 3 hours ago

**The sublime and critical beauty** of Longboat politics
Longboat Key News - 2 hours ago

**Premium Beauty News** - World class news for beauty industry insiders
www.premiumbeautynews.com/ ▾
Premium **Beauty News** provides professionals in the cosmetics and beauty industries with business news on markets and trends, innovations, science and ...

*If you are writing about a popular topic, the news section of Google may show up in regular results. For example, I have written "beauty news" in the regular Google search result and a news section is part of the search, because there is so much content. This will often happen with celebrities or events, meaning readers can see the beauty news without searching for it specifically under Google News.*

If you choose to write news articles, you should expect to be in front of the computer for most of the day. The news industry for celebrities, high-profile events and even red carpets is extremely competitive and you should make sure that you are staying on top of every story that gets published. Your potential page-view count may drop drastically if you are reporting about a news story 24 to 48 hours after it happened. If this is something for you, you should highly consider working towards getting into the Google News program.

# 3.2 Google News

In case you want to explore the Google News program some more, Google does provide website owners with a huge chunk of information on the official Google News program site. If you are new to websites, you may feel completely overwhelmed with the technical jargon in the instructions and guidelines, but a quick Google search may answer many of your questions.

Google may change their guidelines for Google News rather often to make sure that only the best content gets included. They are very attentive when it comes to sorting out evergreen sites from the news program, for example. I can offer you some guidelines as to things you need to keep in mind as you prepare yourself and your blog for Google News, but these guidelines may have changed once you are ready to apply. Before you send in your application for your website, make sure you have met the entire list of requirements on the official Google News program site.

**General Guidelines:**

- You need to write about news; no evergreen articles such as tutorials, how-to articles or advice columns
- You need to learn the important of honest attribution. In other words, you need to state your sources. Like I mentioned previously,

you need to link back to the article where you took quotes from or got the information from. Google won't accept just any type of stories with no credits

- You need to write about content you know. You need to show authority and skills in the subject you are writing about. People can report your website if they find false information

- Google News requires you to have a team behind the website. In other words, they want websites that represent a newsroom. You cannot – as a single individual – apply for Google News. Google wants you to have at least a few writers on board

- Even though it may be common sense, grammar and spelling are of outmost importance in all of your work

**Technical Requirements:**

- The Google News program runs automatically, meaning Google picks up the news article the moment they are published on these pre-approved websites. You need to understand how this program works to get your website ready for it

- All of your article URLs must be unique and have at least three digits in them. In addition, they must be permanent, meaning they don't redirect readers to other sites, such as advertisers

- Each article must have a link (such as the attribution link) that is spread out over several words. A single letter or word may not be enough. Google cannot pick up links that are hidden in JavaScript or pictures

- Only use HTML articles; this is what you are doing in Wordpress

- Since Google uses a program – or robot – to find your newest content, you must allow it to "crawl" your website. This means you must have robots.txt files installed on your website

- Submit a Google News Sitemap to Google once the site is ready for the news program (this is not required, but suggested)

**Quality Guidelines:**

- Just because you know how to spell and write an article doesn't mean that the article is high quality. Google wants you to be honest and professional. You are not allowed to use Google News as a marketing technique or to persuade readers to partake in misleading practices, for example
- You are required to follow basic principles of good journalism and offer valuable and engaging content
- It is all about the readers – remember that one

As you can see, there are many steps and lots of preparation that goes into perfecting your blog for Google News. In addition, Google values websites that have been operational for a while, so you should take it easy and do lots of blogging before even applying for the program. If you don't get accepted, you can apply again after 60 days, meaning you can perfect the issues that should be addressed.

Some people have found great success with their blogging without ever being included in Google News. And it is getting easier to share and promote articles using social media profiles. I will talk more about the power of social media in the next chapter.

However, there is a level of authority that comes with the Google News program. Your website has been approved by someone from the Google team, meaning you are meeting certain standards within the journalistic values that this powerful search engine has put forth. In addition, you could be seen as a powerful beauty brand that is conquering other similar – and smaller – blogs. Of course, there is also the benefit of page views. If you are not in Google News, it could take days before your blog is spotted in Google' search engine. Writing news is a battle you will fight for months and months, but the payout could be excellent. If this is not something for you, you should consider evergreen content.

# 3.3 Evergreen Content

Google News and writing news in general isn't for everyone. Some people who run their own blogs enjoy the freedom of setting their own schedules and writing about content they find appealing – not what the news industry tells them to write. And evergreen bloggers don't have to shut themselves out of the news world. For example, an evergreen article could be comparing two looks from the red carpet. The focus isn't so much on the timing of the red carpet event, but more about the tips and tricks that can be learned from this comparison.

The good thing about evergreen blogging is the freedom – you can essentially do whatever you want as long as it falls under your niche and focus. If you want to talk about a specific hair style that made the news, you can do that without feeling the time constraint of the news standards from Google and other search engines. In addition, you can take an evergreen approach to it, such as compare the hairstyle to others that have been on the red carpet for the past couple of years.

Another benefit is the scheduling of content. You don't have to be in front of the computer all the time. For news content, you have to be on top of your game by checking Twitter, social media profiles, Google News and your Google Alerts to make sure you know when a story breaks. However, evergreen gives you more freedom to build your blog offline. For example, evergreen beauty blogs allows you to build up content at your own speed, allows you to attend industry events where you can get some interviews or information for articles, and even target small companies in your local community for advertising campaigns.

If the idea of being in your office all the time scares you a little with beauty blogging, then evergreen beauty blogging may be for you. You also have the ability to build relationships with other bloggers, since you have more time to get out of the office. The articles you publish in an evergreen structure are applicable for months or even years to come, so you can continue to promote them over time and you can end up gaining some income from the advertisements on the blog articles, because they are continuously ranking well in search engines.

As for evergreen tutorials, you have the freedom to approach them as you please. If you are a writer and feel comfortable writing the tutorials out in steps, then do it that way. "The Beauty Department" has chosen to present tutorials in the form of pictures, but you can also film the tutorials and edit the videos to make the professional and clean. The following are two examples of tutorials from "The Beauty Department."

hair

# RODARTE INSPIRED BRAID TUTORIAL

THEBEAUTYDEPARTMENT.COM'S

## ♥ FAVORITE FALL BRAID ♥

photos above (left: style corn) (right: Kristin Ess)

Earlier this year, Rodarte ruled the runway again. Every beauty site went crazy for the beautifully messy rosette braids. We wanted to do an actual tutorail on how you can get this look and make it wearable for the fall. I love that it's a half up/half down 'do because

*This is an example of a quick hair article from "The Beauty Department" that is partially evergreen article and partially tutorial. You won't find this type of content in Google News, but you will find it in search engine for years to come.*

This is also an example of an evergreen article, which is a tutorial for removing bags under the eyes. This excellent example is from "The Beauty Department," which I mentioned in the introduction. They do an excellent job at making tutorials fun and easy – and evergreen.

Of course, these tutorial videos and picture sequences may take you a while to create if you want them to look as good as these two previous examples. However, you have to keep in mind that these tutorials will be part of a large beauty library that you will create on your blog. You want to show your readers that you make the effort to make it look nice, so your blog becomes a desirable place to visit. In addition, you want to make the effort because an increase in readers means a potential increase in earnings.

In other words, blogging is hard and requires lots of time and effort whether you are doing news blogging or focusing on evergreen content. There is no real right or wrong in terms of how you lay out your tutorials, as long as the information is clean, professional and easy to follow. And remember that you can always change the layout around if you change your mind about your original layout.

You can combine evergreen content and news content on your website if you really want to. It will take more effort on your part because you have to divide the content on your website. Even though the news content can be mixed in on the front page with your evergreen articles, you need to make sure that you are categorizing your news content separately from your other content using the Wordpress category feature. One way to do this is to create a category under your Wordpress posts called "News."

As mentioned under the "Google News" section, Google's program runs automatically, meaning Google picks up the news article the moment they are published on these pre-approved websites. The content must be crawled by the Google robot, and if you get approved for the Google News program, the articles the robot picks up must be news only.

One way to make sure this happens is to install a robots.txt plugin on your Wordpress panel. You can find this free plugin under the "Plugins" page and edit it via your "Widgets" page once it is installed. Here, you can select what posts should be crawled by Google News when you publish new content and what should be considered for the regular search engine. Having your news articles under one category makes this step much easier.

Of course, you need to set up this plugin before applying to Google News, but you won't see your news articles in Google News before being approved. If this is the approach you want to take, you should be prepared to invest a lot of time and energy into your blog. You would need to stay on top of the news world to get the latest news on your website, but take the time to create some strong tutorial articles as well. Even though it is possible to start this type of blog as a single person, it is recommended that you start building up your team for your blog so you don't have to do it all on your own. And remember, Google News requires you to have a team behind you.

# Chapter 4: Social Media Marketing

Now that you have a good idea of what you want your beauty blog to be, you need to think about how you can share the content so you can get some readers. Even though you have spent lots of time creating news articles or evergreen tutorials, you won't make a profit if you don't find readers. A decade ago, websites would have to compete with readers in search engines, send links out via newsletters and even try to share information with people offline in hopes of getting more page views.

These days, many websites and blogs are using social media platforms to share content, especially links to articles. As you can imagine, news websites and gossip websites are often sharing links – sometimes up to 20 to 30 times – if not more per day. Each article written gets tweeted out or shared on Facebook, but large content mills only share the odd article that could potentially create some discussions. As a beauty blog, you need to make sure that you have a presence on the big social media marketing networks. At present time, Facebook and Twitter are rather effective for sharing content, so you should create a business page on Facebook and a strong profile on Twitter to represent your beauty blog. Of course, you are representing your blog on these networks, so there are some etiquette rules you should follow to remain professional and protect your beauty brand. The following chapter will give you a brief introduction to social media marketing and how it is beneficial to your beauty blog.

# 4.1 Setting up Twitter and Facebook

Most people seem to have a Facebook profile these days and it is one of the fastest growing social media networks online. It started out being open to just students with the goal of sharing everything, but it has grown into a large sharing platform between individuals, companies and celebrities. You may already have a Facebook profile, meaning you know the ins and outs of Facebook. However, for your blog, you should create a page that people can like and follow – not a profile with a friend request system.

You should not create your Facebook or Twitter profiles before you have decided on a name, and a general look for your blog. Of course, you want your Facebook page and Twitter profile to match the general look of your blog, so people can recognize them when they are searching for them. You want the profile picture to be the logo or the name of your blog, and you want the cover picture to be a representation of your blog. For your beauty blog, you have plenty of options. If you are focusing on hair blogging, your cover picture should capture your hair niche. Or, if you are doing a cosmetics blog, you can have a cool eye-shadow picture to captivate your readers. It all comes down to branding.

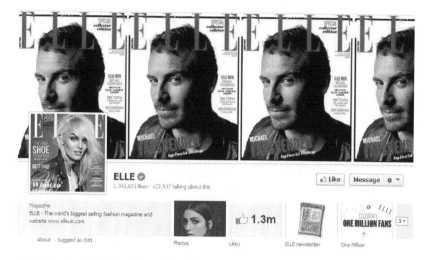

*This is what Elle's official Facebook page looks like. Even though the profile picture isn't the official logo, the name is indeed both on the profile picture and the cover photo. Since Elle has been verified by Facebook as being the official page for the magazine, it has a blue tick next to the name.*

As you can tell, Elle has truly branded the profile to represent the magazine. As a reader, you are not in doubt that you are visiting the official Elle Facebook page. You can see the current month's magazine cover, see pictures of models and celebrities and even get links to the official website. It is all about branding and recognition.

The same thing is true for the official Elle profile on Twitter. As you can see on the next page, the Twitter profile has the logo of the business as the profile picture and it has a captivating cover image that makes you think of fierce fashion and beauty. I have also included a snap shot of two tweets so you can see how Elle shares links to the official website.

Of course, the goal of social media marketing is to attract readers. The more readers you have, the more clicks you are likely to get. And with the clicks come the potential for more advertising revenue. In other words, you want to work towards making an impression on social media platforms because this is where your target audience may be hanging out. It may take a while to find them, but once you do, you can expect them to stick around if you are offering valuable and useful content on your blog.

*This is the official Twitter profile for Elle in the US. The profile picture is indeed the name of the magazine, while the cover photo is a fashion-forward picture from a recent photo shoot. In addition, the links color is the same as on the website.*

The top question I get in regards to social media marketing is the amount of updates or tweets you should be sending out on a regular basis. On a daily basis, you should share what is new on your blog in the forms of tweets and updates. For example, if you have a goal of sharing 10 new articles or videos on your beauty blog per day, then make sure you share all of them on your social media networks. Make sure you space them out, so people are constantly reminded of your blog. If you share them all at once, people may forget the name of your blog within a few hours. Sharing the links throughout the day reassures you that your readers are reminded of your blog on a continuous basis.

Now that you have your two social media profiles somewhat planned out, let's take a look at what you need to do to get the readers coming your way and what you need to do to keep them there.

# 4.2 Online Marketing Tactics

There are hundreds of profiles and pages on both Facebook and Twitter. Many of these will have competitors. And as a beauty blog, you know you already have a few competitors. You may have plenty of experience in your niche and know that you have some strong competitors that you will need to stand apart from. Social media marketing is all about making an impression and these platforms give you space to differentiate yourself.

So how do you get readers to come your way compared to going to the sources they have been following for years? Well, there are a few techniques you can try out repeatedly to see if you can get more followers on Twitter and more likes on Facebook. I have provided a list here with a brief discussion for each point.

- **Ask Questions**: You want to make your readers are thinking about the things you are posting. You also make them want to question their actions. For example, you may be promoting a new product on your blog because your readers have voted it the best product for wrinkles, for example. You want to encourage people to buy the product through your website, so you can get a share of the purchase through your affiliate program (more on this in the next chapter). To get readers' attention, you want to question why they haven't tried out this new product, considering the high reviews people have been giving it. You always want to have the answers when posing questions

- **Giveaways**: People love free things and you may be able to attract some new readers by having a contest or a giveaway based on a certain set of rules. For example, you may have a sample product from a company that you were reviewing. You want to give it away to one of your readers. But be wise about a giveaway; you want that person to work for it. For example, you may give the product away to the person who re-tweets your Twitter account the most times over a given period or has shared your professional blog page on Facebook the most times. Here, you are getting free marketing in return

- **Recognition**: Over time, you may find that you have the same people writing comments on your page or replying to tweets on your Twitter account. These are people who are highly interested in your blog and are eagerly waiting for the new blog posts to be released. Chances are you will recognize them after a while. Another marketing tactic is to give recognition to these individuals. If they share your status update on Facebook or re-tweets your tweet on Twitter where you give them recognition, your blog name may be seen by their respective followers and friends

- **Content**: Sometimes, it isn't all about hair or makeup. You want to share content that people will actually click on and explore. If they don't click on the links you share on social media, chances are that you won't be making much money on the blog. You have to share content that is intriguing and captivating to your readers

- **Introduction**: Facebook and Twitter allows you to write a brief introduction to the content you share with your followers. For example, you can introduce your content vaguely and ask a question, which will prompt people to click on the link you have shared in hopes of finding the answer. You don't want to give it all away in your updates, as people may not feel the need to click on the link to find the answer. It is your duty to get these readers to your blog

- **Discussions**: Even though you may be annoyed with the amount of notifications you will get on these networks, you want to encourage discussions on your social media profiles for two reasons. For one, the more people talk using your blog Twitter handle in the tweets or Facebook page in status updates, the more exposure you will get. Second, the more people come back to comment, the more clicks you may end up getting. You don't necessarily have to participate in the discussions if you don't want to

# 4.3 Things to Avoid

As you are posting things on Twitter and Facebook, you may find that people are talking about your blog and some comments may be negative. Don't let one or two people bring you down. There are plenty of negative people in the world, so don't give them the time of day. However, since your actions on your social media profiles do reflect on your blog, there are some things you should keep in mind if you do plan on saying or doing something against rude readers.

For one, you don't want to get too personal with your readers. For example, you don't want to share something from your private life if you are trying to align your beauty blog with the big ones on the market, such as Elle.com. "The Beauty Department" has been branded by the two girls who created the blog, which is an approach you can take. But you don't see these girls posting things from their private lives. In other words, don't post a picture of your dinner last night. Celebrities may be doing it, but you don't see companies getting personal like that.

Another ineffective technique is to share something that has nothing to do with your niche. For example, many people will tweet or post something from a sponsor that has little to do with their brand or mission as a famous individual. You don't want to get sponsors that are trying to sell something completely irrelevant to your blog. Your readers may be questioning your motives if all you post is from a sponsor. You can easily scare readers away if it looks like you are all about the money you are earning from your readers – not about the readers' interests. And once you lose your loyal readers, it can be tough to get them back.

Lastly, you should monitor your pages – not get involved. As mentioned previously in this chapter, people can be mean. Chances are you will have followers or people who will not get along with everyone. You may spot some arguments or heated discussions on your pages, but you should not get involved. You should only step in if someone contacts you about someone's behaviour or if you find that someone is crossing the line with comments that could be considered sexist, racists and so forth. You want to either block the person or contact them privately. Don't become involved in something you don't need to deal with. And if you do have to get involved, do it where others cannot see it. It is much more professional to deal with these issues in private.

# Chapter 5: Monetizing the Blog

At this point, you know how to start your blog by building your own website. You know how to customize it to make it what you truly want it to be using the features offered by the theme you purchase. You know where to find your content, the pros and cons of writing both news and evergreen content and you have learned some techniques when it comes to social media marketing. Now you need how to make your blog profitable, so you can make some money and start making a career out of your beauty blogging.

One of the most common advertising programs online is Google's own Adsense program. It is easy to set up on your beauty blog and start earning money, but you will have to have a website ready before you apply for an account. But many websites use this program and perhaps you want to try something different. As mentioned earlier in this book, you could also go out and find companies that would want to advertise on your website. And lastly, you may use your popularity to get yourself some higher paying advertisers. I'll explain each of these approaches in this chapter.

# 5.1 Adsense

Google Adsense is one of the most popular advertisement programs online for bloggers. It is used by many bloggers around the world. Some of the biggest blogs around use Google Adsense, but many new blogs that have less than 10 readers per month also implement Google's ads. So, how does Adsense work? Essentially, companies pay Google a certain amount of money to advertise their products on various websites. By signing up to Google Adsense, you are essentially saying that you want some of these ads on your page. Every time someone clicks on an advertisement, you make money – except you can't ask people to click on the ads. Each advertisement will give you a certain dollar amount. For example, one ad click may earn you $3 while another may give you just $0.02. It all depends on how much the advertiser has paid for the ads. And as a blogger, you cannot see what ads are worth more.

Now, you may be worried about what kind of advertisements you will get on your website. You don't want something that infuriates people or insults your readers. This is where the importance of keywords and niche content plays a huge role. Google uses the content you have provided on your blog to find relevant ads for your site. For example, if you are blogging about cosmetics and beauty, you may find that you have advertisements for lip gloss and wrinkle cream. While the ads may not be completely specific to your niche, they are within the same industry. Blogs that try to cover too many topics will often end up with random ads, such as website development, food services and weight loss.

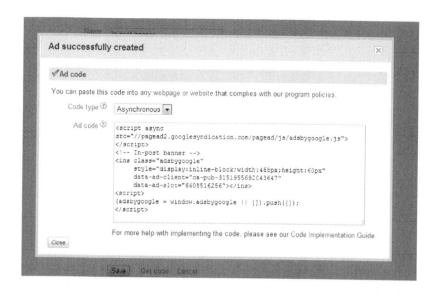

Google Adsense does give you the freedom to create all types of ads. You can create text, video and image advertisements. If you have lots of images on your pages, then image ads may blend in better, which could encourage more clicks, for example. Once you have chosen your format, you will get a code, which you can copy and paste into plain HTML text (in a post or a page) or in a text box under your "Widgets" if you want an ad in your sidebar.

| Estimated earnings | | | | Finalized earnings Details » |
| --- | --- | --- | --- | --- |
| $0.00 ⑦ | $0.00 | $0.00 ⑦ | $0.00 | $1.38 ⑦ |
| Today so far | Yesterday | This month so far | Last month | Unpaid earnings Prior to Nov 1, 2012 |

You will be able to track your clicks and earnings almost immediately. It is not quite real-time, but you should have a good idea of how the ad placements are working for you daily. You can also see how many dollars you are making per 1000 or per 10,000 page views.

Remember, you can implement advertisements in the articles themselves, in the sidebars of your blog and even as part of your blog layout. When you first install Google Adsense, you will see some yellow boxes where the ads are supposed to be. During the first installation, Google needs time to determine what topic you are writing about and what keywords you have used the most on your blog. These yellow boxes should be removed and replaced with advertisements within an hour or so. If you are worried about your readers seeing these yellow boxes, make sure you implement the advertisements late at night, so fewer readers see them.

# 5.2 Pre-Paid Advertisers

Pre-paid advertisements are similar in appearance to Google ads, but the progress of getting the ads onto the website differs greatly. Pre-paid advertisers are the business owners in your local community who fit your niche. These business owners could potential buy advertising space on your blog, which is a pre-paid agreement between you and the business.

For example, one person may be trying to sell her homemade soaps to people with sensitive skin. You could tell her that your beauty blog focuses on skin products, remedies and problems, meaning all of your readers could potentially be interested in the product. Since you have 30,000 viewers daily, for example, you can guarantee her that she will get at least 30,000 sets of eyes on her advertisement per day if you place the ad on every page and article you have published. The ad could be designed by the business owner, so the logo and business name is included in the advertisement.

This way, you can create an advertising package where you decide how much you want to charge for your traffic. For example, you decide how much you want to charge for a monthly advertising campaign, where 30,000 views per day are guaranteed. The price should also take the size of the ad and repetitive placement into account. Create a payment plan, where you can get the money up front for a set period of time, such as a week or a month. This pre-paid advertisement plan could get you some serious income and could help you build relationships with applicable business people in your local community. And you have control over the design aspect, since you want the ads to meet your design standards on your beauty blog.

*These are two examples of pre-paid banner advertisements that you could implement on your blog. These are taken from Google Adsense ads, but you could make the ads look as you please. If you have a design standard for advertisements, make sure you give examples of how you want the advertisements to look. It is your blog and you want to protect your blog's image and brand.*

You essentially set your own rules with pre-paid advertisements. You just have to keep the advertisement up for an agreed period of time and make sure to collect payment. You can create the additional details for your agreements as you please.

# 5.3 CPM Advertisers

As your blog starts growing in content, you may see your readership grow as well. The more content you add to the blog, the more readers may be coming your way. You can track your readers using Google Analytics, which you should install during your website set-up phase. You want to make sure you have the correct number of readers from the first day. You also want to be able to track popular content, so you can see what your readers enjoy reading and sharing. Even though you may have started out with just a few hundred readers, you could see it growing quickly as people start sharing your content on social media networks. However, if you are thinking about this from a business perspective, you won't be happy with

5000 viewers per month. You want to pursue upwards of 50,000 views per day and increase your income from advertisements.

As mentioned previously, you do get an increase in page views when you are included in Google News and getting more views does have an advantage – CPM. While Google Adsense relies on people clicking on the ads for you to make money, CPM advertising (cost-per-thousand impressions) pays you based on how many views you have on your website. Readers don't have to click on the advertisements for you to make money. There will be a set rate based on one thousand impressions. In other words, the more views you get, the more you could potentially earn.

You would definitely benefit from larger advertisers, such as CPM businesses, if you are gaining thousands of readers per day. If you are interested in pursuing this type of advertising, do a simple search online to see what programs are available to you. Most of these businesses will offer ideal advertisers for your beauty website, but you have to prove a large readership to be considered. These programs may change frequently, so make sure you do some research to see which programs have the highest cost-per-thousand impression rate. You can combine both Adsense and CPM programs on your blog if you please.

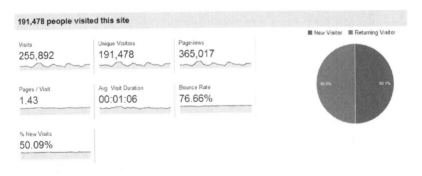

*Sometimes you may have to use your page views to show potential advertisers how many readers you have on a daily basis. The higher the visitor count, the more you could potential charge a pre-paid advertiser for a spot on your blog. In addition, you will have to prove your page view count to CPM programs using a trusted analytical program, such as Google Analytics (shown here).*

# Chapter 6: Building Your Brand

Many bloggers are happy with just writing articles every week and promoting them continuously to get a certain amount of page views and earnings each month. The internet may change over time, meaning you could see a drop in page views on occasion. At times, Google will change the algorithm for searches, so your website may be moved up or down in search results. In other words, it is good for a blog to have other means of income as part of building a bigger brand. You want to secure yourself financially. As many will say, building a brand cannot be done overnight. You should only consider these brand extensions when you are ready to grow your blog. It takes time to make online growth successful.

In this chapter, I will outline three different ways to expand your blog into a brand. All three methods allow you to keep the beauty brand you have created, but provide you with a possibility of making more money. While these methods may take time to create and perfect, you are creating a larger online beauty brand and opening the door for earning opportunities.

# 6.1 Adding a Magazine

One branding opportunity is to create a beauty magazine that goes hand-in-hand with your blog. Elle.com started out as a magazine, but started doing beauty blogging because the industry changed slightly. Now, Elle makes money through magazine sales and possible advertising spots online. Even though you have a beauty blog, you can do a magazine that adds value to your brand.

For example, if you are running a tutorial blog where you offer tutorials on eye makeup or hair styles, you can create magazine issues that focus on these tutorials. You don't have to have a monthly issue, like Elle or Cosmopolitan. You can create a magazine issue that focuses solely on certain hair braids, for example. You can do niche issues that are evergreen issues rather than monthly issues. You control your brand.

Many people often associate starting a magazine with spending money. Everything involved with creating a magazine costs money; hiring writers, paying for photographers for images, paying for designers to plan and outline the magazine, and paying the printers to get copies of your magazine. At this point, you have invested lots of money in the magazine without getting a dime back because you haven't made a single sale yet. However, there are programs available for you to save some money on the magazine production.

Since you are creating the magazine out of inspiration from your blog, you may already have the content in mind. Since you shouldn't sell the same tutorials in your magazine as you share on your blog for free, you should create original content for your magazine. Your blog readers may buy your magazine because they want more information than what you are offering online for free.

**Publications in Dark Beauty Magazine**

**ISSUE 25 - Families & Furs**
Digital Download -
http://bit.ly/DBM_25 Featuring content from Aalia Oursbourn, Jason Bassett, Kevin James, Denyse Rizzo , Greg Desiatov, H. James .

Ⓘ Standard / 8.25" x 10.75"
▣ Print: $64.95

**Dark Beauty Magazine**
**ISSUE 24 - Wicked Fun**
Digital Download -
http://bit.ly/DBM_24b ISSUE 24 – Wicked Fun features Jus Vun, Andrea Pede, Andrew Hiorth, Jessica Prautzsch, Karyne Bond,...

Ⓘ Standard / 8.25" x 10.75"
▣ Print: $64.95

**Dark Beauty Magazine**
**ISSUE 24 - High Fashion**
Digital Download -
http://bit.ly/DBM_24 ISSUE 24 – High Fashion features Mana Baranova, Askar Ibragimov, Bénédicte Manière, Garjan Atwood, ,

Ⓘ Standard / 8.25" x 10.75"
▣ Print: $79.95

**Dark Beauty Magazine**
**ISSUE 23 - Fall '13**
Digital Download -
http://bit.ly/DBM_23 Featuring Breaking Bad star RJ Mitte! Editorials and stories from Jacco Breedveld, Marilin Saar, Temira .

Ⓘ Standard / 8.25" x 10.75"
▣ Print: $64.95

*This is an example of a beauty magazine called "Dark Beauty Magazine" that is printed and sold on MagCloud – a magazine printing platform offered by Hewlett Packard. Since HP prints your magazine for you on-demand, you don't have to buy hundreds of copies in advantage. It is free for you to create a magazine issue and put it on sale.*

Using print-on-demand for your magazine can help save you money. As discussed above, you are the expert in your chosen field, meaning you and some guest-bloggers can create unique content for your magazine. Your guest-bloggers may require their usual fee, but they get additional exposure. You don't have to hire additional writers. In addition, you can take your camera to a local store or a product showroom to take a handful of professional pictures for the magazine.

Of course, starting a magazine takes time and it is very different from starting a beauty blog. As you are planning a magazine as part of your brand expansion, there are some other things you should keep in mind.

- **Magazine Name**: You need to come up with a name that suits both the magazine content and your beauty blog. You need to make sure your blog and the magazine are linked. The obvious choice is to use the same name as your blog and use the same font and color for the logo, so people can easily recognize the magazine

- **Content Development**: As discussed earlier, you need to make time to create content for your magazine that is exclusive to the magazine. You cannot take blog posts from your website and print it in your magazine and expect people to pay money for it

- **Print**: HP MagCloud will print your magazine issues when a purchase is made. You don't have to print several copies and do the sales yourself. You don't even have to deal with customers, as HP handles the sale, the transaction, the printing and the shipping. You just get money sent to your PayPal account as a royalty payment

- **Distribution**: You do have to think about where you want to distribute the magazine. HP will sell the magazine directly through their website and online store, but you can promote the sales link on your blog, your social media profiles and through interviews with other blogs. You are responsible for marketing your magazine

## Formats: Standard

HP MagCloud allows you to create your own magazine from a PDF document. You can simply create your magazine in a Microsoft Word document and then save it as a PDF file. As long as all fonts are embedded, you can have your magazine in the HP printers in mere minutes – at no cost to you.

At this point, there are other print-on-demand services available to you that you could use, if you find that HP doesn't offer you the look and price point that you were looking for. However, it is recommended that you use print-on-demand for your magazine until you see the sales potential. If you can see that the magazine is selling well, you could switch to a cheaper printer where you purchase the magazines yourself and distributing them yourself. Buying in bulk may be cheaper than print-on-demand.

# 6.2 Writing E-Books

If you find yourself to be more of a writer, you can expand your brand by selling downloadable e-books through your blog to make money. The content of these e-books could be the same as in your magazine, for example. You may want to publish a book about hair braids or one about applying dark eye makeup to get the perfect smoky eye.

If you plan on writing e-books for your blog, you should know that you are responsible for writing, editing and distributing the blog. Of course, you can ask people to edit the books for you if you want to have a second pair of eyes on them before you hit the publish button.

You have two options for your e-books; you can sell them directly on your blog using PayPal's shopping cart option. You will have to set up this shopping cart system yourself, but PayPal has plenty of resources to help you set everything up. Your readers can download the e-books after purchase directly from your blog. If you choose this route, you are responsible for addressing transactions that fail with your buyers.

The other option is to use distributions to sell your e-books. There are advantages and disadvantages to this approach; the disadvantage is that it requires more work because you have to get ISBN numbers for each book before any distributor will pick it up. However, some distributors such as Smashwords and Amazon have nationwide and worldwide coverage, meaning your beauty brand could essentially become known all over the world. Even though it is a bigger investment in terms of the ISBN number *and* making the e-book an official book rather than a downloadable PDF file, you could see bigger returns on both sales and blog exposure with larger distribution.

# 6.3 Affiliate Stores

If you don't have time to create a magazine or the energy to write e-books, you could pursue affiliate sales to expand your brand and make some money. Affiliate marketing has been addressed earlier in this book and it works well with beauty sites that offer product reviews. Affiliate marketing is straight forward; it has the same business model as Google Adsense. You are essentially using your blog as a marketing platform for other companies. However, you can be more selective as to which products you want to share.

For example, you want to sell the products you are offering reviews for on your beauty blog. Or maybe you just want to sell the best hair products from a high-end line. Amazon Affiliates allows you to choose the products you wish to display in your online store. You can even create categories for the product, such as "fragrances" and "lotions," for example.

You make money every time a product is sold on Amazon via your blog. In other words, you don't make money every time the product is sold on Amazon. The buyer has to come from your website and complete the sale in order for you to make money. It is essentially a referral system. You are marketing products for Amazon and you get a percentage of each sale made on Amazon through your account.

In other words, the products you select for your blog must be very applicable to the content you are sharing. And adding a store just for the sake of making money may end up backfiring on you, if you don't make a conscious effort to integrate the store into your blog. For example, if you integrate a certain product into a blog post that boasts about how awesome this particular product is, then the reader is more likely to make a purchase through you. If you just add the store as an afterthought, the sales numbers may not something to brag about.

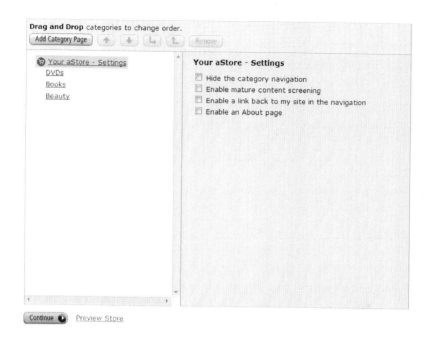

*This is a screen shot from Amazon's affiliate program called "Amazon Associates" in Canada and "Amazon Affiliates" in the US. Here you can create a store that contains products from Amazon that suits your niche directly. You don't have to sell products that don't appeal to your target audience.*

If you already have an Amazon account, you can set up your Affiliate or Associates store immediately. The setup is rather straight forward and you will get a few questions about your location and your tax information, so Amazon can make sure that the payments are handled in time without any withholdings later on.

As you are creating your store, you will be able to go through the products offered through Amazon. You will have to search for them manually, so make sure you know the names of the products you wish to feature. If you are selling high-end products on your beauty blog, your credibility may rise with your readers, because you are showing that you understand your industry. Be very selective with the products you are choosing to represent on your blog, as poorly reviewed products should not be endorsed by you.

If you are uncertain about a product, you can check out the Amazon website to read through any product reviews offered by users. You can choose whether you want the reviews to be visible on your website, which could be a good thing if you are choosing to sell very popular products. But just remember to keep the products within your niche. You don't want to appear money hungry.

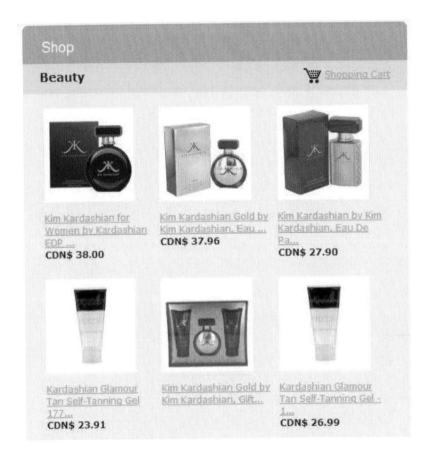

*This is a screen shot of an Amazon store on your website. You can customize the link color and products as you please. You can also choose the layout and have a sidebar with a shopping cart, so people can see what they are buying and how much they are spending. Everything is operated via the Amazon website.*

If you find that you are not making any sales through your blog, you could try to integrate the products more effectively into your content. You don't have to have a product review blog to make it worth your while. For example, if you are offering tutorials, you could sell brushes, hair elastics and even books on hair braiding if that was your focus. You need to think like a salesperson – where a sale is possible, a sale is possible.

# Chapter 7: Hiring New Writers

If you are thinking about doing everything mentioned in this book, including starting a blog that talks about beauty news as well as evergreens, offering products through Amazon, and selling e-books through worldwide distributors, then you will be one busy beauty blogger. As websites grow and gain more readers, the owners or editors will often start finding contributors or freelancers to write content for the sites on a continuous basis.

These freelancers and contributors are not like the guest bloggers discussed in previous chapters. Guest-bloggers will often write one or two blog posts on occasion, but aren't necessarily interested in investing lots of time on your website. If you find that you could use a couple of writers to help boost your content and your readership, then hiring some new writers may be the ideal thing to do. You will have a hard time finding people who are willing to write for free, but you may be able to find people who are willing to work for the advertising revenue that the articles bring in, hence a share of the content revenue. If you find that you have a little bit more money to play around with, you should be able to find writers who are willing to work for a flat rate.

# 7.1 Contracts

Hiring new people is exciting. You get to interview them and inquire about their experience and best of all you get to grow a team for your beauty blog. With twice as much energy and production, your beauty blog may reach new heights within a short period of time. However, you should always protect yourself when you are planning on hiring new people for your blog.

Since you own your beauty blog, you are essentially the boss over everyone you hire. These writers may have the freedom to write about stories they find interesting and applicable, but they have to adhere to your standards. And there must be a level of respect between yourself and the writers you hire.

It is always a good idea to protect your blog from the very beginning. You don't want to deal with a writer who is going against your wishes or demanding a higher pay. You want to outline all expectations, payment guidelines and content standards in a contract prior to the writer starting the work. The purpose of the contract is to have clear guidelines in place and have clear expectations about what you want and about what the writer can give.

There are a few things you should consider adding in your contract. You want to point out an exclusivity clause that protects your blog from copied content. The writer you hire is expected to write original content that will only appear on your website – nowhere else online. In addition, the writer is not allowed to copy other people's articles online and use them to their own benefit on your website. You have to outline the rules and make sure that they all understand what the rules are and what will cause you to terminate their contracts. You can never really predict how writers or contributors will react over a period of time, so the best thing you can do is protect yourself in a professional manner. If you find that people are using you, then don't hesitate to let them go. You don't want someone to ruin your beauty brand because you didn't address these issues in time.

# 7.2 Plagiarism

Plagiarism is a continuous problem in the online world. It is rather simple to just copy and paste an article from one website and add it to your own. One could imagine that this would save a lot of time and effort, but plagiarism – the act of stealing someone else's work – is indeed illegal. And Google doesn't handle stolen content well. Since everything is done automatically at Google, the system is very quick to pick up copied content. Sites with copied content are often downgraded in the search engines, meaning your page views could take a nosedive.

It is important that your readers understand that plagiarism is not allowed on your website. Plagiarism hurts not only the site your writer took the content from, but also your own. You want to make sure that your blog only has unique content. One way to do this is to run new articles through a plagiarism scanner online before allowing a person to publish on your behalf.

These scanners are free and will pick up a string of words used elsewhere and redirect you to the scraped website. You will be able to judge whether the article was indeed copied with ill intention or if it was a common phrase that triggered the program to pick up similar stories.

You will never be fully able to protect yourself completely. You can't control what other writers are doing online, including copying your articles without giving you any credit for the work in question. However, as your blog grows and becomes a big credible beauty brand online, more people will realize that smaller bloggers are probably copying your content rather than the other way around. You don't see Elle.com being accused of scraping content from smaller blogs that cover similar topics. With growth and credibility come a sense of trust and establishment, meaning plagiarism may be handled more professionally – and hopefully occur less frequently.

# 7.3 Protection

However, the written content is just one thing you will have to worry about. Another issue that online writers and websites have to deal with is the issue of pictures. Surprisingly, you will rarely find an image online that doesn't belong to someone else. When you do a random search for a beauty wallpaper picture for your blog, for example, someone may claim ownership over the pictures you are browsing through. It is the same for pictures used on all articles, blogs and so forth.

Some companies have made millions selling usage rights to pictures of celebrities that the paparazzi have snapped in major cities, such as New York, Miami and Los Angeles. As a blog owner, you cannot use these pictures just because they fit your blog content. They belong to someone else and you often have to pay large sums of money to use them.

While you may be taking your own pictures for your blog to save money, you have to make sure that the writers you hire for your blog understand these rules, as people tend to just copy and paste images without thinking about the repercussions. They are using images without permission and since that is indeed stealing, legal action could be taken to protect the images and retrieve lost profits. And you don't want to be the person responsible for footing that bill when it comes in the mail in the form of a lawsuit.

To protect yourself, it may be wise that you provide the images for the blog posts submitted by users until you find a viable solution for images. One way to do this is to use images submitted by people on social media websites, such as Instagram and Twitter. Some people may be thrilled to share their pictures as long as they get referenced, so don't be afraid to reach out and ask for permission.

In addition, you want to check the titles of your articles by searching for them randomly in search engines to see if other websites are copying your titles – or if your writers are copying pre-existing works. Also, be very active on social media as readers will point out every flaw that you show. So, if one writer is caught copying another website's work, people will call it out. Listen to people on your social media profiles, because they are going to brutally honest whether you like it or not. And this honesty could help secure your success.

# Conclusion

Now that we have come to the end, you may feel a little overwhelmed if you haven't started your blog at all. You may be thinking about a name for your blog still because you wanted to see where this book took you before you made any concrete plans. And that is quite alright. In fact, beauty blogging takes lots of planning if you want to make money from it eventually. As you may have learned from this book, making money online comes down to a certain trust between website owner and readers. If you don't have your readers, then you won't be able to have a functional blog that will eventually make you some money and perhaps put you on a career path within the blogging world. So, it is important that your readers should come first – in any and every case.

As you were reading this book, you may realize that there is more to the beauty industry than just selling products and teaching people how to do things, such as create the perfect fishtail braid. In fact, you can educate others, share your creative tutorials, build a reputable brand and make money online. You are essentially building a business with your blog because you are thinking about your daily operations with your blog posts, thinking about finances with your advertising income and paying potential freelance writers and about product development and brand expansion as you tackle e-books or magazines.

Hopefully, you will look at blogs more critically now as you start researching for your own blog. Look at where successful beauty blogs place their Google advertisements, for example, or examine blog titles to see which ones are more captivating than others. You can learn quite a bit by just browsing through other blogs that are similar to your own.

Before I end this book, I just want to briefly go over the main points that we have discussed in this book, so everything is fresh in your mind as you put down this book and get ready to create your beauty empire.

- **Setting up the Website:** After reading this chapter, you may be not questioning why a free blog isn't good enough. As discussed, you need more freedom with your website and you don't need a hosting company grabbing the valuable advertising space and essentially profiting from your hard work. Instead, invest the time and effort into creating a functional and modern website that will give you everything you need to make your beauty blogging dream a reality

- **Finding Content:** Stealing is a big no-no in the online world, both for pictures and for articles. In this book, I've revealed some techniques to get the stories on your blog without stealing the content from elsewhere. The key is to write original content surrounding the quotes or pertinent information, while crediting the source you are using for the information. Honesty is the best policy

- **News vs. Evergreen:** After giving you a brief introduction to Google News, you may be searching for big news websites online to see how they are indexing in Google News and what stories are making it to the top of the search results. However, as discussed in the book, it is very hard to get included in Google News and you should not give up on beauty blogging if Google rejects your application. Many bloggers are making it work by sharing the content using social media profiles and going directly to the readers. You can still have a successful news blog without being included in Google News. It may just take a little more work on your part

- **The Power of Social Media Marketing:** Don't underestimate the power of a 'like' or a 'follow.' Every reader counts and should be treated as a person, not a number. Since so many people use Facebook and Twitter on a daily basis, you could essentially reach hundreds of people every day using the right titles, hash-tags and encouraging content sharing. Your presence on social media could essentially help determine your success rate

- **Expanding the Brand:** Beauty blogging may be something appealing to you on a low scale, but people who dream about running the next big beauty blog may be thinking like a business owner; expansion, expansion, expansion. The key to expanding online is your niche; you don't want to leave it. Everything you add to your blog or brand must suit your niche, so you don't lose your audience. If you feel you can't do that, then you may be better off not expanding your beauty brand. If you are in doubt, ask people around you who understands your vision and your plans for the future

- **Making Money:** Of course, blogging for a living wouldn't be possible without making some money and paying the bills. The reality is that blogging of any kind is hard, especially if the goal is to make a lot of money. Income from blogging takes time because money comes from credible content. Content becomes credible over a period of time and you may find yourself making pennies or dollars in the first few weeks. But the more time and effort you put into your blog, the more earning potential it will have

- **Hiring People:** Lastly, you want to think about growth and teamwork. It may be a scary thought to hire people, especially if you don't know them personally. However, the reality is that the larger beauty blogs online are not operated by a single person. A large team is often behind the blog, meaning more content is created and more branding and marketing is done. You need someone with you along for the ride, especially as your beauty blog grows over time

In conclusion, I just want to add that you are now thinking like a business person and because of that, I want you to start off on the right foot. In all of my blogging books, I add a business plan to help you get started on the right path and this book is no exception. I force you to answer questions that will only benefit you down the road. I wish you all the best in your beauty blogging endeavours and I look forward to seeing what you have created.

# Appendix: Sample Business Plan

A well-structured business plan covers seven major aspects of starting, operating, marketing and financing a business. The seven sections include 'executive summary,' 'business description,' 'market strategies,' 'competitive analysis,' 'design and development plan,' 'operations and management plans,' and 'financial components.' You should complete each section to ensure you are on the right track and fully prepared when you launch your e-business. If you do run into problems while planning, research options to find a possible solution. Chances are that you do have several options available to make your dream website a reality.

# Executive Summary

Commonly, the 'executive summary' section follows the e-business plan's title page and should serve as a summary of everything discussed in the business plan. In other words, this single page should convey exactly what you want with the business, how you plan to obtain it and how you will finance it. Since you only have a single page to convey all of this information, you should only state the facts – not explain *how* you will use advertisements or *how* you plan to obtain guest writers. If the reader wants more information, he can reach the other sections for more detail. Although this page goes immediately after the title page, it is easier to write it after the entire plan is done, so you get all of the important information onto that single page.

# Business Description

This section is essentially a large, detailed description of what your e-business is. Is it a blog or a magazine? What services or products will be offered? For one, you want to do some research regarding the industry where your niche falls. That means you want to explore the food and wine industry for your chef's blog, or explore web design if you want to do an online community for professional designers and coders. Some of the things you must identify in the plan include:

- Are you selling a product (book, information products, etc) or are you offering a service (online community, blog with advertisements, etc)?
- Will you be manufacturing your products yourself or will you be selling them for others through affiliate programs?
- Is the business new or do you already have a brand in place?

- Are you running the business as a corporation or a sole-proprietorship? Both are business structures which must be registered with your local town or city.
- Running your e-business professionally could lead to some tax benefits
- Will you have guest contributors, online community members or will you be doing all the work yourself?
- Who are your distributors and resellers? Are you planning on selling your products on your website alone using the PayPal e-commerce system or are you planning on using Amazon's distribution channels for your self-published products, for example?
- Identify your products: what are they, how large is your product line, where will they be sold, how much will they cost to produce and what is your profit margin?
- Identify your services: what are your services, what are you planning to offer your readers for free, what services are offered for a price and what is the profit margin?

Profits are everything in any business. You cannot sell a product for the production price or any lower price, because you will be losing money and fast. In fact, it could mean that your business will be gone within months because you don't have money to pay your bills or create more production. A healthy profit margin is around 50% and anything higher is both beneficial and risky. It is beneficial for you because you get more money in your pocket, but risky because a high-priced product may not sell as well.

Create a chart that will explain how much each product or service will cost you to produce and add the profit margin. You can decide to profit margin based on your expertise or background. If you are writing books, information reports or magazines, for example, your profit margins may be set based on how much the printing and distribution costs are.

In addition, explain how your business will be profitable in comparison to other bloggers or e-businesses that are offering services or products within your industry. Use your niche angle to find a selling point that stands out and explain why people would want to choose your products over your competitors. All of this information will help you in your marketing materials and the design of your website. If you can get your selling point across quickly, you may become more successful and profitable.

# Market Strategies

This section requires you to analyze the given market you are getting into. Now, this does not mean you have to analyze the e-business market. This means you have to analyze the market your niche falls into, such as the healthy living industry, the food and wine industry, the crafting industry or the do-it-yourself industry. This is because you are getting advertisers from this industry and you will be reaching target markets within this industry. Some things you should research include:

What is the size of the market in terms of buyers? Are these markets looking for a solution you can offer with your niche products or affiliate website? Who falls into your target market? Is it busy parents, stay-at-home mothers, do-it-yourself persons, entrepreneurs, or students? Identify your target audience by narrowing down geographic location, customer attributes or product-orientation. Some products may be better suited for men than women, for example.

Identify your projecting market share: what are your distribution markets, the prices per products and your placement on the market? Will you fill a void in the market?

What are the sales potentials? Is there a demand for your products or knowledge on the market, or will your blog just add to an already saturated market?

# Competitive Analysis

As mentioned in the first chapter, it is important to research the market to determine who your competitors are before starting a niche blog or e-business. You don't want to start something that has already been done, simply adding to an industry that already has plenty of products. You may just be a small business competing with the big guys. The benefit of doing a competitor analysis is finding their flaws, so you can cash in on those. You want to fill the voids in the industries with your niche, not copy something that has been done already.

- Identify your competitors and determine their sales angle. What are they experts in? What is their niche angle? How do you differ from them? What are their sales numbers and what are their flaws? Some sales are made public, so examine where these websites or companies make the most profit
- What are your immediate competitors' strengths? Why are customers coming to them for products?

One way to identify your competitors' strengths and weaknesses is to create small profiles for each competitor. A competitor's strengths and weaknesses are usually based on the presence and absence of key assets and skills needed to compete in the market. When doing the profile, answer the following; the reasons behind successful as well as unsuccessful concepts or products, prime customer motivators, and successful products offered by the companies.

To create a competitive profile for your e-business, create comparison charts for the following; products, distribution, pricing, promotions and advertisements. In one column, describe what your competitors are doing in each area, and in a second column, identify your strategies. Find your selling points and how you are better than your competitor.

# Design and Development Plan

This section of the business plan covers anything and everything related to how the business will operate. If you are planning on operating the e-business on your own, you should still complete this section, as you need to manage everything from content to finding advertisers. There are three sections on this chapter you need to cover:

- **Product Development**: How often will you produce new products, such as books, magazines or information products? Remember, customers like reliability, so if you publish a monthly magazine, ensure the magazine is ready each month. Set a schedule that suits your daily business tasks. If you are running a niche blog, have publishing times identical each day. Use the automated publishing option, if possible.

- **Market Development**: How do you plan on spreading the word about your business? Are you planning on using SEO strategies to get your products or blog posts indexed in search engines? Do you have plans on using social media, such as Facebook and Twitter, to create a buzz about your new website? Create a marketing plan with ideas, which you can implement at different times during a single year.

- **Organizational Development**: How will the business operate on a daily basis? Are you producing everything yourself or do you have guest writers who contribute content on a daily basis? Will you have a development budget in place that allows you to hire writers after a certain income level has been reached?

# Operations and Management Plan

The operations and management section of your business plan is different from the design and development part, because operations focus on the on-going operations of the business. The development plan may describe how you plan on having writers working for you, while the operations plan will focus on how often you plan to offer work, issue payments and hire new writers. The business operations should discuss your operating expenses involved in operating the business. Of course, you have to pay for hosting and your website theme, which is a one-time cost. Hosting is a single payment once per year. Any additional domain name is around $20-$30. Any payments for writers should also be included in the operating expenses involved in the business, even if you are only getting help in researching content for your informational reports. You should also discuss how the business will operate in terms of marketing and sales, production, research and development and administration.

- **Marketing and Sales**: Create an on-going marketing plan that will explain short-term goals and long-term goals. Each marketing tactic you plan to use should have a goal of increasing sales, so make some estimates as to how much your sales level will increase. For example, a Twitter marketing campaign may sell 50 more copies of your book than your average sales. Sales and marketing go hand-in-hand. Don't forget to include income from advertisers or subscriptions
- **Production**: Production has to do with how much you plan on creating in terms of new products per month or year. Blog posts should be created more often than full-length books, for example.

Creating a production plan will help you stay on track with your publishing

- **Research and Development**: No business survives without doing some industry research, as a single industry may change drastically in a short period of time. Whether you are in the crafting industry, the do it-yourself industry or work with food, you must examine what is hot, what is trending and what people are buying. Give yourself at least a few hours per week or month to examine what is popular in your given field. One way is to use Google Alerts for keywords relevant to you, so you get emails directly to your inbox about what people are talking about and what is in demand
- **Administration**: The administration part of the business is one part that may take up much of your time, unless you are organized. Administration includes everything from getting advertisers, handling payment options for advertisers and guest writers, handling hosting and web design, controlling quality, meeting budget expectations and sending emails to new potential advertisers. If you can create a well-organized schedule, the administrative part of running a business doesn't have to take up much of your time

# Financial Components

This last part of the business plan involves creating a financial plan that works for you. The financial plan includes a functional budget that gives you some wiggle room in case you do lose some advertisers along the way, but also gives you room to grow. If you do have more than one income stream, it is a good idea to keep them separate and do financial statements at the end of the fiscal year to examine how each income stream is functioning. If you are earning the majority of profits from book sales but only mere dollars from advertising, perhaps spend more time on producing books than searching for new advertisers.

One of the things you must consider is creating income statements. In other words, these statements tell you how much you earn per product or per advertiser per month. You know exactly where the money is coming from at any given time. In addition, you can use this information to see if your marketing tactics work, as sales may increase tremendously after certain marketing campaigns. Income statements will also let you know if you are earning a big profit or losing money each month. To summarize what should go on an income statement, here is a comprehensive list from *Entrepreneur.com*.

- **Income**: Includes all the income generated by the business and its sources.
- **Cost of goods**: Includes all the costs related to the sale of products in inventory.
- **Gross profit margin**: The difference between revenue and cost of goods. Gross profit margin can be expressed in dollars, as a percentage, or both. As a percentage, the GP margin is always stated as a percentage of revenue.
- **Operating expenses**: Includes all overhead and labor expenses associated with the operations of the business.
- **Total expenses**: The sum of all overhead and labor expenses required to operate the business.
- **Net profit**: The difference between gross profit margin and total expenses, the net income depicts the business's debt and capital capabilities.
- **Depreciation**: Reflects the decrease in value of capital assets used to generate income. Also used as the basis for a tax deduction and an indicator of the flow of money into new capital.
- **Net profit before interest**: The difference between net profit and depreciation.

- **Interest**: Includes all interest derived from debts, both short-term and long-term. Interest is determined by the amount of investment within the company.
- **Net profit before taxes**: The difference between net profit before interest and interest.
- **Taxes**: Includes all taxes on the business.
- **Profit after taxes**: The difference between net profit before taxes and the taxes accrued. Profit after taxes is the bottom line for any company.

Of course, an income statement will only inform you of how much money you are pulling in each month. It doesn't necessarily tell you of how much you are spending or whether your budget is balanced. A cash flow chart will show you exactly you are spending money in as well as how much you are earning. In other words, the chart will inform you of your current financial standing at any given time.

Examples of what needs to go on a cash flow statement can be seen below in the list created by *Entrepreneur.com*.

- **Cash sales**: Income derived from sales paid for by cash.
- **Receivables**: Income derived from the collection of receivables.
- **Other income**: Income derived from investments, interest on loans that have been extended, and the liquidation of any assets.
- **Total income**: The sum of total cash, cash sales, receivables, and other income.
- **Material/merchandise**: The raw material used in the manufacture of a product (for manufacturing operations only), the cash outlay for merchandise inventory (for merchandisers such as wholesalers and retailers), or the supplies used in the performance of a service.
- **Production labor**: The labor required to manufacture a product (for manufacturing operations only) or to perform a service.

- **Overhead**: All fixed and variable expenses required for the production of the product and the operations of the business.
- **Marketing/sales**: All salaries, commissions, and other direct costs associated with the marketing and sales departments.
- **Loan payment**: The total of all payments made to reduce any long-term debts.
- **Total expenses**: The sum of material, direct labor, overhead expenses, marketing, sales, G&A, taxes, capital and loan payments.
- **Cash flow**: The difference between total income and total expenses. This amount is carried over to the next period as beginning cash.
- **Cumulative cash flow**: The difference between current cash flow and cash flow from the previous period.

Of course, not everything on this list will apply to your business, as you may not have a loan or production labor. Create your cash flow chart as it applies to your specific e-business. If you need additional support in creating your financial statements, visit *Entrepreneur.com* as this website has free resources and comprehensive articles on financial development for any kind of business.

Printed in Great Britain
by Amazon.co.uk, Ltd.,
Marston Gate.